Classical Northern
Wu Style Tai Ji Quan

Denise,

TaiJi

Forever!

Frank Allen
+
Tina

Tina C. Zhang

Classical Northern Wu Style Tai Ji Quan

The Fighting Art of the Manchurian Palace Guard

Tina Chunna Zhang **and** Frank Allen

BLUE SNAKE BOOKS
BERKELEY, CALIFORNIA

Published by Blue Snake Books/Frog, Ltd.

Blue Snake Books/Frog, Ltd. books are distributed by North Atlantic Books, P.O. Box 12327, Berkeley, California 94712

Cover and book design by Susan Quasha

Printed in the United States of America

Blue Snake Books publications are available through most bookstores. For further information, call 800-337-2665 or visit our website at www.northatlanticbooks.com.

PLEASE NOTE: The practice of martial arts and the meditative arts may carry risks. The instructions and advice printed in this book are not in any way intended as a substitute for medical, mental, or emotional counseling with a licensed physician or healthcare provider. The reader should consult a professional before undertaking this or any other martial art, movement, meditative art, health, or exercise program to reduce the chance of injury or any other harm that may result from pursuing the instructions and advice presented in this book. Any physical or other distress experienced during or after any exercise should not be ignored, and should be brought to the attention of a healthcare professional. The creators and publishers of this book disclaim any liabilities for loss in connection with following any of the practices, exercises, and advice contained in this book, and their implementation are at the discretion, decision, and risk of the reader.

The Chinese character on the half-title page is *wu*.

ISBN 13 978-158394-154-6

Library of Congress Cataloging-in-Publication Data
Zhang, Tina Chunna.
Classical northern Wu style Tai Ji Quan: the fighting art of the Manchurian palace guard / By Tina Chunna Zhang and Frank Allen.
p. cm.
Summary: "Classical northern Wu Style Tai Ji Quan teaches the traditional formwork and fighting skills of imperial banner guard, preserved by the students of Yang Lu Chan, who guarded the Emperor in Beijing"—Provided by publisher.
ISBN 1-58394-154-1 (trade paper)
1. Tai chi. I. Allen, Frank. II. Title.
GV504.Z55 2006
613.7 148—dc22

2005037890

1 2 3 4 5 6 7 8 9 UNITED 12 11 10 09 08 07 06

Popularize Tai Ji Quan Around the World

CALLIGRAPHY BY MASTER LI BING CI

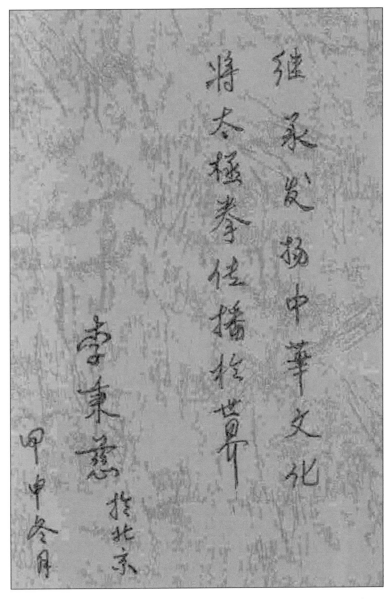

Preserve and Develop Chinese Culture

CONTENTS

Wang Mao Zhai (1862–1940)

Wu Jian Quan (1870–1942)

Yang Yu Ting (1887–1982)

Wang Pei Sheng (1919–2004)

Li Bing Ci (1929–   )

Preface

Tᴀɪ ᴊɪ Qᴜᴀɴ, ᴀʟsᴏ ᴋɴᴏᴡɴ ᴀs ᴛᴀɪ ᴄʜɪ, has attracted people from all walks of life since it was introduced into Chinese culture more than four centuries ago. This art has become an important and beneficial regimen in the daily lives of people around the world.

In the twenty-first century, the popularity of this traditional Chinese martial art has grown due to its ability to improve one's quality of life. As a perfect exercise for people of all ages and all physical conditions, tai ji quan plays an important role in our modern society by promoting well-being, minimizing stress, and helping to achieve the goal of a longer life.

The different styles of tai ji quan are a part of the art's charm. Many generations of masters devoted their life to practice, research, and transmit the essence of the art to their students. This book will introduce classical Northern Wu Style Tai Ji Quan, which was created in Beijing, China by its founder Wu Quan You (1834–1902). This form has been traditionally practiced and passed down by the masters of Northern Wu Style Tai Ji Quan and it maintains all of the original techniques, without modification by later generations. We hope this book will help to preserve the culture and traditions of the art as well as provide an access to information on this unique style of tai ji quan.

Chapter 1

Introduction to Tai Ji Quan

The yin-yang symbol, which represents the classical foundations of Chinese philosophy is known as tai ji—the supreme ultimate. The outline circle symbolizes the whole universe. The curvature within the circle symbolizes the opposite, yet interdependent, nature of yin and yang. The black yin and the white yang teardrop shapes, shown in a sort of embrace, symbolize the balance of yin and yang. The dots show the concept that yin and yang do not exist purely individually, and there is always some yin within the yang and some yang within the yin.

Tai ji quan, with a name meaning "supreme ultimate fist," was originally developed as an internal martial art by simple country folks. (See Chapter 3 for more information on internal martial arts.) Over time, tai ji quan has taken on great significance, embracing many facets of Chinese culture such as classical philosophy, traditional medicine, self-defense, and physical exercise. It mixes a philosophy of living with an understanding of the human being. Balance of defensive and offensive movements is an essential ingredient. Folk martial arts were used as combative forms for competition, for performance, and for catching thieves or self-protection. The emphasis is on individual combat, and training focuses on the individual's development of technical and physical skills. Its purpose is to defeat or capture an opponent, or to avoid being hurt by an opponent. The techniques focus primarily on empty-hand martial postures, but the art does contain weapons training; typically, the weapons employed are sword, broadsword, and long spear. Some early tai ji quan professionals earned their living by performing on the streets. Those with excellent skills had a chance to become imperial guards or trainers.

Tai ji quan practitioners use its special techniques to cultivate their *qi*, or life force energy, and strengthen the *yi*, or mind intent, to make their bodies and minds strong and to be able to use tai ji quan's fighting principles to develop their skill in combat arts. Every movement or posture in tai ji quan has an application for self-defense. For several hundred years after its birth, this folk art has traditionally been passed on by successive generations of the founder's family members and their disciples, as well as by great teachers around world. As a martial art and internal body control system, tai ji quan has long been popular for people to practice as a health art for the mind, body, and spirit. More than forty million people in the world today

1

practice tai ji quan daily to maintain their health, and a small percentage of them also enjoy practicing the fighting techniques of the art.

Tai ji quan has never been presented as a simple physical exercise. With the concept of yin and yang in harmony as its philosophy, the principles of traditional Chinese medicine as its root, and with its forms and postures correlating with the acupuncture points and meridian channels, tai ji quan is the perfect practice for people to exercise every part of their bodies externally while exercising their inner organs to help keep a good balance in their health and daily lives. Its unbroken flow and continuous movement internally provide great health benefits by building strength, restoring balance, increasing flexibility, and reducing stress. Practicing tai ji quan will improve the coordination of one's physical movements, boost the immune system, slow the aging process, and develop energy. It uses gentle aerobic movements and specific postures to build a healthy spine and flexible joints while improving coordination. By cultivating qi, or life force energy, in one's body, tai ji quan strengthens the immune system, regulates the circulatory system, clears the respiratory system, and balances the nervous system in order to maintain the practitioner's general health.

Tai ji quan is a gentle, non-impact exercise that provides basic healthy living benefits such as improved physical movement to achieve fitness and to attain the proper weight, balanced emotions, and the release of stress from the nerves and mind, along with the development of qi. Tai ji quan is practiced in slow motion for learning self-control of both mind and body. Moving in slow motion gives a person the needed time to feel deeply in the body. Slowing down helps a person become aware of and in control of mind and physical movement. Tai ji quan uses the shifting of a person's weight back and forth and left and right to feel, find, and control the balance of body movements, allowing the practitioner to regulate the circulatory system without stressing the respiratory system. The gentle, non-impact movements, specific postures, and routines of tai ji quan practice will build and keep excellent balance, a healthy spine, and flexible joints, while smoothing away the pain and old injuries, both physical and emotional. The relatively slow motion of tai ji quan practice perfectly promotes relaxation by encouraging a relaxed mood, relaxed body, and relaxed concentration. A calm mind is always a basic living tool that leads to happiness and success. Medical and scientific studies have proved tai ji quan's healing effect on various diseases, especially chronic diseases. For maintaining a person's overall health, preventing illness, and living to an advanced age, tai ji quan practice is perhaps one of the best exercises for people of all ages and physical conditions.

The beauty of tai ji quan is expressed by the human body's natural, unforced movement, the healthy body alignments, and the smooth transitions between postures. The longer a person properly practices tai ji quan, the stronger the mind and body become and the more likely that the goal of longevity will be achieved.

A Short History of Tai Ji Quan

The art of tai ji quan was created in the mid-1600s during the time of the fall of the Ming Dynasty and the rise of the Manchu Dynasty, known as the Qing. During this time of social upheaval a number of martial arts were created to help people deal with the problems of their daily lives. Cities were under the protection of one government or another, but country villages were left to their own devices when it came to protecting their crops and the communities from roving marauders. Chen Village in Henan Province was just such a village and, as with many others, the men formed a village defense force with which to protect homes and families.

Two stories recount how the Chen family's long boxing became tai ji quan. One simply states that a local martial artist, Chen Wan Ting, had become a great general for the Ming, but when the dynasty changed, he returned to the village of his birth. Upon his return he began to train his fellow villagers in the martial innovations that he had developed during his years of military service. These innovations, when combined with the village's traditional long boxing, became Chen Family boxing, later known as tai ji quan. Another somewhat more popular version of the creation of Chen Style tai ji quan tells how in this same time period of the mid-1600s the men of Chen Village were practicing their long boxing when a stranger who was traveling by stopped to watch. When they asked him what he thought of their art, the stranger said that he could see that they were working very hard, but unfortunately they were putting their efforts into an inferior style. The villagers immediately took umbrage at the stranger's remarks and challenged him to display his superior martial art to them. One by one the stranger effortlessly disposed of the village's best fighters until the men of Chen Village begged the stranger to teach them this mysterious art of his. The stranger told them that he was Wang Zong Yue, a Ming loyalist; as such, revealing his art might reveal his whereabouts to the Qing officials, but he could teach them the secrets of his art and how to apply it to their own long-fist system. Wang Zong Yue stayed in the village long enough to accomplish this and when he disappeared from the village and history he left behind an art that would evolve into Chen Style tai ji quan.

Chen Family boxing continued to develop in the village as a family secret for the next couple of centuries. Chen Chang Xing (1771–1853) organized the style into a first form and a second set known as cannon fist, Chen Yu Ben simplified Chen

Chang Xing's teachings into a new form, and Chen Qing Ping created the small-frame style of Chen Family boxing.

The art stayed in Chen Village until Chen Chang Xing decided to allow his loyal bond servant Yang Lu Chan (1799–1872) to become his disciple in the Chen Family martial art. Yang had become a servant of the Chen family at age ten and worked hard and long for the family. Because the youngster exhibited both an interest and a talent for the art, Chen Chang Xing taught him all of the Old Style Large-Frame Chen Family boxing. (Note: Large-frame forms move like machines with small fast gears on the inside and large powerful gears on the outside. They are noted for their large sweeping movements. Small-frame forms move like machines with large powerful gears on the inside and small fast gears on the outside, and are known for their small, explosive movements.)

Yang's bond was completed when he reached the age of forty and at that time he returned to his home in Yong Nian County in Hebei Province. There he lived in the Chen family's pharmacy and began to teach his martial art to a few students. The most talented of these students was a local landlord's son, Wu Yu Xiang. Wu and Yang became friends over the course of Wu's training and eventually Wu decided to bring Yang to Beijing and introduce him to his older brother, who worked as a minister for the central government at the capital. Yang Lu Chan and his new martial art became popular in Beijing and, after winning a number of challenge matches both with spear and empty handed, Yang developed a clientele of wealthy students. Martial arts enthusiasts in the capital were especially impressed with Yang's ability to convince an opponent of his defeat without killing or seriously injuring him, even in spear matches.

Wu Yu Xiang returned home and realized that his generosity had left him without a martial arts instructor. He decided to travel to Chen Village and study with Chen Chang Xing to complete his martial education. On the way he stopped at a village where Chen Ching Ping was teaching his Small-Frame Chen Family boxing; Wu Yu Xiang decided to stay and study the small-frame art. When he had absorbed the teaching of Chen Qing Ping and returned to his village, Wu found a surprise waiting for him. While he was away, one of his brothers had discovered a manuscript in a salt shop; the manuscript contained the martial arts secrets of Wang Zong Yue, who had taught the Chen family how to internalize their long boxing two hundred years earlier. Wu Yu Xiang combined what he had learned from Yang Lu Chan and Chen Qing Ping with the information in the manuscript to create his own style of martial art. Today this art is sometimes referred to as Old Wu Style tai ji quan, but more often is known by the name of Wu's student Li's student, a master Hao—Hao Style tai ji quan.

Hao went on to teach his art to Xing Yi Quan and Ba Gua Zhang master Sun Lu Tang, who then created Sun Style tai ji quan. (Note: Xing yi quan is a distinct internal martial art, different from both tai ji quan and ba gua zhang. Sun Lu Tang was a, perhaps *the,* first master of all three arts. As an author in the early 1900s, Sun was the "father" of the idea of tai ji quan, ba gua zhang, and xing yi quan being one family known as the internal martial arts.)

Wu Yu Xiang's salt shop manuscript is today called the Tai Ji Quan Treatise and forms the major section of classical tai ji quan.

Meanwhile, Yang Lu Chan's fame and popularity had reached such a height in Beijing that he was hired as the martial arts trainer of the guards of the Imperial Palace (today known as the Forbidden City). Yang Lu Chan's best students were his sons Yang Ban Hou and Yang Jian Hou. As soon as they were old enough, the boys began to help their father teach the guards at the palace. Also, when Yang Lu Chan heard that his student Wu Yu Xiang had created some refinements in the art he immediately sent the older son Yang Ban Hou back to Yong Nian County to study with Wu Yu Xiang and bring these refinements back to Beijing and into the Yang family art. This art had now acquired the name of Yang Family tai ji quan.

When Yang was first trying to popularize his art, the philosophy of Taoism was having a resurgence in the capital. Yang's martial art, powered by the principles of Taoist energy work, now became known as *qi gong.* Pointing out the Taoist roots of his art was simply good marketing, so he named the art after the grand ultimate principle of the harmony of yin and yang, tai ji. He also created a tie to ancient Taoist history for the art by choosing Taoist alchemist and philosopher Zhang San Feng of the Yuan Dynasty as an ancient patriarch for tai ji quan. The Yangs created the story of Zhang sitting by his hermitage on Wu Tang Mountain and observing a battle between a crane and a snake that inspired him to create the soft martial arts predecessor of Yang's tai ji quan. The Taoists monks on Wu Tang Mountain heard this legend, thought it embodied a fitting metaphor, and promptly developed their own tai ji quan with lineages dating straight back to Zhang San Feng.

When Yang Ban Hou returned to Beijing after studying the small-frame form with Wu Yu Xiang, he resumed his duties helping his father train the guards at the Imperial Palace. Ban Hou was also building his reputation as the finest empty-hand fighter of all tai ji quan. While his brother Jian Hou carried on their father's tradition of the tai ji quan spear duel, Ban Hou exemplified the art with empty hand, defeating the infamous "dog boxer" and the strong man known as the "Man of 10,000 Pound Strength" with a single technique for each of them. Later in his life Yang Ban Hou also dispatched a young Shao Lin boxer, making the young man sing like a swallow with his last breath. Needless to say, Yang Ban Hou was revered among the palace guards and the best of them studied with him as well as with his father. In this group the best of the best were Wan Chun, who mastered the yang or harder aspects of tai ji quan, Ling Shan, who mastered the yin or softer elements of the art, and Quan You (1834–1902), who mastered the transformational energy of tai ji quan, which allowed him to switch smoothly from yin to yang and practice what was considered the highest level of the art.

The fame of the Yang family and their tai ji quan continued to grow. Yang Jian Hou's sons Yang Shou Hou and Yang Cheng Fu became well-known teachers. Shou Hou carried on the small-frame style of his uncle Yang Ban Hou and was also known for his empty-hand skills and quick temper. Yang Cheng Fu popularized the large-frame style and was one of the masters to first present the idea of tai ji quan as not just a fighting art, but a health art with benefits for all people. He had thousands of students and spread the art to many parts of China. His student Cheng Man Ching and Man Ching's top students, William Chen and Benjamin Lo, were the pioneers of Yang Style tai ji quan in America.

The Manchurian Imperial Guard Quan You taught his tai ji quan to three main students: his son Quan Jian, who when the Republic replaced the Manchu Dynasty in 1912 adopted the Han name Wu Jian Quan (1870–1942); Wang Mao Zhai (1862–1940); and Guo Fen. After teaching for a while in Beijing, Wu Jian Quan relocated to Shanghai where he founded a strong Wu Style tai ji quan school that still exists today. He modified his father's form slightly and created a few trademark postures of his own. Eventually he left the Shanghai school to his son-in-law Ma Yue Liang and his daughter Wu Ying Hua. These two led the Shanghai school into the new millennium, as both lived well into their nineties. Ma Yue Liang's student Sophia Delza gave the first-ever public performance of tai ji quan in America when she demonstrated her form at the United Nations building in New York City in 1956. Upon leaving Shanghai, Wu Jian Quan moved to Hong Kong, where he founded another strong Wu Style tai ji quan organization. When Wu Jian Quan passed away in 1942, the Hong Kong school became the domain of his sons Wu Gong Yi and Wu Gong Zao. Wu Gong Yi modified his father's form into a version that is uniquely his, and he and his brother made the style very popular throughout Southeast Asia. Much of this popularity stems from Wu Gong Yi's 1954 challenge match with a much younger white crane stylist. The Hong Kong tabloid newspapers had promoted the event and loudly questioned whether tai ji quan was still a fighting art or had been watered down to simply a exercise program for the promotion of health. When the typical-looking middle-aged man Wu managed to bloody his twenty-years-younger opponent's nose and garner a draw decision, he was considered the savior of tai ji quan in southern Asia. Although Wu Gong Yi's Hong Kong form and the Wu Jian Quan set practiced by the Shanghai school are quite different, they have still collectively become known as Southern Wu Style Tai Ji Quan.

Wang Mao Zhai continued to teach Quan You's tai ji quan in Beijing until his death in 1940. This form remained basically unchanged throughout this time. Wang Mao Zhai's top student was the prodigy Yang Yu Ting (1887–1982). Yang began his tai ji quan training at a very young age and was teaching the art while still in his teens, with the blessing of his master, Wang Mao Zhai. By the time of his death in 1982, Yang had been teaching the tai ji quan form of his master for more than seventy-five years. His most well-known students are Wang Pei Sheng (1919–2004) and Li Bing Ci (1929–present). In the 1980s Wang Pei Sheng created a 37-Posture Wu Style short form and taught this style in many parts of the world. Also in the 1980s Li Bing Ci headed a committee that developed a 45-Posture Wu Style Tai Ji Quan set incorporating the basic postures of Quan You's original tai ji quan form with a number of the trademark postures of his son Wu Jian Quan. Li Bing Ci has also to this day continued to teach Quan You's original empty-hand and sword sets to Chinese and foreign students in Beijing. Through the efforts of Wang Pei Sheng, Li Bing Ci, and their many students, the Northern Wu Style of tai ji quan is finally being made available to tai ji quan practitioners around the globe.

Tai Ji Quan As a Health Art

Tai ji quan was not originally invented or practiced by people for health, but rather as a fully developed martial art. But the concept of tai ji quan as an exercise that is practiced for developing energy and strengthening mind and body has always existed, and should not be ignored. It is a modern innovation to practice martial arts for health and longevity—this is the purpose for most people who practice tai ji quan today. The Chinese internal martial art of tai ji quan has the same kind of natural healing power as the traditional Chinese medicine techniques of deep tissue massage, acupuncture, and herbal remedies. These arts are all based on the same culture and medical theory, sharing the same foundations discovered and developed by scholars and common people who practiced various cultural arts through many generations in China. Chinese people used movement to cultivate the human body's qi, or natural energy, to prevent and heal illness before medicines had even been formulated.

Using movement and posture to cultivate the energy in the body has long been documented in Chinese history. Through the Spring and Autumn and Warring States periods (770–221 B.C.), a method called daoyin evolved for promoting health and curing certain diseases by combining regulated, controlled breathing

with physical exercises. The silk scroll discovered in the Western Han dynasty (206 B.C.–25 A.D.) tomb at Mawangdui, near Changsha, Hunan Province is covered with more than forty human figures. In different postures, outlined in black and painted in color, these figures have been identified with the earliest Chinese system of exercise to improve one's health. The ever popular daoyin—today's qi gong—exercise "Five Animals Frolic" was created by the famous Chinese physician Dr. Hua Tou in the Eastern Han dynasty (25–220 A.D.). He researched and observed animal movements and then, combining this knowledge with the relationship between the five elements and the five major internal organs, Hua Tou created the oldest medical qi gong form, which he used for healing others and for keeping himself healthy. That may be why tai ji quan has so many names of animal movements to signify its postures. Dr. Hua Tuo's inventive work had a far-reaching influence on the later development of physical exercise for improving health and for therapeutic purposes. During the Song (960–1279) and the Ming (1366–1644) dynasties, there appeared several exercise routines, including the still popularly practiced qi gong form of Baduanjin, or Eight Pieces of Brocade, and Yijinjin, or Muscle Change Classic. Some of the qi gong and tai ji quan popularly practiced as tools of alternative healing in hospitals and among workers in modern China have aspects that are rooted in these ancient qi gong systems. History tells us that these early qi practices were the fundamentals that were collected and developed to create the forms of tai ji quan. Therefore many experts consider tai ji quan to be one of the highest levels of qi gong. Knowledge and theory of the meridian channels and acupuncture points in the human body is a contribution to the world from the Chinese and, as tai ji quan combines this knowledge in its practice, it functions as perhaps the best medicine available. The natural medicine of tai ji quan comes from the human body itself and emphasizes the flow of energy in the human body as a power to maintain general health and prevent disease.

Based on modern theories of anatomy, sports physiology, and biomechanics, some experts have found that the practice of tai ji quan can also minimize mental and emotional stress. Since much of what we identify as illness is caused by unbalanced mental health, learning how to control the emotions with the ideology of Eastern medicine expressed through tai ji quan becomes a major reason for many people to practice tai ji quan. The yin-yang philosophy of tai ji quan is a lifetime study that helps a person to approach all matters with an eye toward balance. This leads the practitioner to the path of a happy and healthy life. No matter what one's purpose or motivation to learn the art, regular practice of tai ji quan restores the natural balance that people may have lost in certain periods of their life, either mentally or physically. Simply practicing the gentle, rhythmic movements, natural breathing, and body-mind coordination of tai ji quan brings the same, or perhaps better, health  benefits through the movement as receiving a massage or maintaining a healthy condition with herbs, because tai ji quan does the same thing that Chinese medicine generally does—open the meridian channels to enable the energy flow through the entire body, including the brain, and to circulate the blood in a stronger and more balanced manner. Traditional Chinese medicine theory is the root of tai ji quan, which moves in a soft, fluid, and gentle way to cultivate and generate qi in the body, to balance or release the accumulated tension or blockages in the muscles, tendons, and organs of the body, and enhance the function of the network of one's health system.

That is why more and more people practice tai ji quan as a part of healthy lifestyle to cultivate more energy in their bodies, to promote well-being, and to achieve an illness-free and long life.

Tai Ji Quan As a Martial Art

Through most of the first three centuries of its development, tai ji quan was practiced, taught, and thought of solely as a martial art.

At the time of its inception in Chen Village during the mid-1600s, tai ji quan was simply an improvement and advancement in the methods used by the men of the village to protect their families, homes, and crops. When Yang Lu Chan left Chen Village for Beijing in the mid-1800s, he brought with him an advanced and refined martial art that embodied the unique ability to defeat an opponent without crippling or killing him. It was Yang Lu Chan's ability at showing this unique martial skill in a series of challenge matches that led to his becoming the trainer of the Imperial Palace guards. His sons Yang Ban Hou and Yang Jian Hou assisted Yang Lu Chan in training the palace guards, and both became respected fighters in their own right. The younger Yang son, Jian Hou, followed in his father's footsteps as an unbeatable master of the long spear. His ability to stick to an opponent's spear with his own and then deflect the enemy's spear point back to its place of origin and often into its owner's flesh was considered uncanny. Jian Hou's sticking ability was such that he could hold a bird in the palm of either hand and have the bird seemingly be stuck there by lowering his palm and neutralizing the bird's attempts to push off for flight. Older brother Ban Hou was the best empty-hand fighter ever produced by the tai ji quan style. While still a teenager he met the challenge of a famous "dog boxer" and left the older martial artist semi-conscious in the dirt and bleeding from several orifices. Bragging of the event to his father brought him a demoralizing dose of chastisement, which led Ban Hou to rarely ever speak of his later challenges. In the silence of his remaining years Ban Hou still managed to quietly lay a few more fighters to permanent rest.

Among their palace guard students, the Yang family developed three outstanding martial artists. Wan Chun developed a high level of ability of *Fa Li*, the yang, or outward, aspects of tai ji quan. Ling Shan was known for his skill in strength of *Liu*, the drawing-inward techniques of the art. A guard named Quan You was the best student of the Yang family and, by studying arduously with both Yang Lu Chan and Yang Ban Hou, Quan You became adept at the techniques of switching from outward, hard energy to inward, soft energy. This was known as transformational energy and was considered the highest level of the Yang family art. All three of these men were hardened Manchurian warriors whose job was to protect the persons, possessions, and real estate of the royal family.

Quan You's top students were his son Wu Jian Quan and another student known as Wang Mao Zhai. Upon Quan You's death, Wang Mao Zhai continued the traditions of Quan You's martial art in its birthplace of Beijing. Wu Jian Quan moved south and, along with Yang Jian Hou's third son Yang Cheng Fu, developed the concept of tai ji quan practice as a health art. This development brought thousands of students to these masters and made them rich men. Even though Wu Jian Quan and Yang Cheng Fu became the fathers of tai ji quan as a health art, both of these masters were also known for their martial skills.

Even as the fame of tai ji quan as a health art grew, tai ji quan continued to maintain its reputation as a martial art. In 1953 Wu Jian Quan's son, Wu Gong Yi, entered a ring in Macao as a paunchy, middle-aged tai ji quan master facing an athlete twenty years younger—a semi-professional ball player, trained in a couple of martial arts. When Wu caused an unstoppable nose bleed in his young opponent and garnered a draw decision with this technique, he was hailed in southern Asia as the savior of tai ji quan's reputation as a martial art.

With the advent of the experimental approaches of the 1960s, tai ji quan became famous as a movement art as well as a health art. Sadly too, the disappearance of the martial arts aspects of tai ji quan took place during the Cultural Revolution in China. But some masters still practiced the martial techniques in their backyards and passed them on to their students in China. In this manner, the art continued its reputation as a traditional Chinese fighting art.

Tai ji quan is a whole "system." When people study tai ji quan, they should study it completely, in all its aspects, rather than just for its martial, health, or movement aspect alone. It is especially important to include the aspect of fighting that made the art, and from which the rest of aspects come. The tai ji quan principles can only be gained through experiencing the fighting applications, for which the graceful movements of tai ji quan were invented.

Tai ji quan study develops the mind through the practice of physical self-defense techniques; this is an important element of the art. No one can become a great tai ji quan practitioner without understanding the martial application that each posture was originally designed for. Not being martially trained in tai ji quan practice means that the practitioner has ignored or lost the traditions of the art—the meaning of the movements or postures has most likely been replaced by a dance-like appearance and are no longer deeply related with *jing, qi, shen* (essence, energy, spirit), which are basic requirements of tai ji quan. As in other styles of martial arts, tai ji quan practitioners develop confidence and skill in fighting. But tai ji quan is famous as well for its neutralization skills—for soft overcoming hard, and the ability to use four ounces of one's power to deflect a thousand oncoming pounds. This type of training makes tai ji quan a unique and exceptional fighting art.

The development of weaponry has advanced and often replaced physical skills in combat, but not all crimes today involve the use of a weapon. Self-defense is a necessary skill in the modern world. The confident mind-set and techniques of tai ji quan must be learned to attain the martial aspects of the art and be able to use them in daily life. The other advantage of learning martial arts through tai ji quan is that it fits people who never martially trained in their younger years and find it impractical to start external martial arts training when they are older. It is never too late too begin and continue to practice tai ji quan. This allows people to develop martial ability at an advanced age.

CHAPTER 2

NORTHERN WU STYLE TAI JI QUAN

NORTHERN WU STYLE TAI JI QUAN history is a part of the history of tai ji quan that originated with members of the Chen family. The Chen family lived in Chen Village, Chenjiagou, in Henan Province, for generations. Chen Wang Ting invented a boxing style with softness, circularity, and internal force. The family kept the boxing within the family until the time of Chen Chang Xing (1771–1853), who accepted Yang Lu Chan as a student. The Chen family kept a low profile and practiced in the village until Chen Fa Ke began to teach in Beijing in 1928.

Chen Wang Ting

Yang Lu Chan (1799–1827) was from Yong Nian County, in Hebei Province. He went to Chen Village in search of livelihood. He learned Chen Style tai ji quan from Chen Chang Xing. After returning to his hometown, Yang passed the art on and was eventually appointed martial arts instructor to the imperial banner battalion, in the capital city. He modified the original Chen family form, making it gentler in order to teach it to more people, and founded what became known as Yang Style tai ji quan.

Northern China gave birth to many styles of martial arts, most notably the internal martial arts of tai ji quan, ba gua zhang, and xing yi quan. These arts were invented and developed in northern China. Many martial artists were trained, gathered, challenged, and exchanged skills in the northern part of China, especially in Beijing, where the royal family hired the most highly skilled martial artists to guard and train the officials in the palace.

Yang Lu Chan

When Yang Lu Chan taught tai ji quan in Beijing, Wan Chun, Ling Shan, and Quan You were his three top students. Wan Chun had the hardest Fa Li, Ling Shan threw people the farthest, and Quan You had the best neutralizing skill. Later, Quan You developed his own tai ji quan style, a transformational form that came to be called Wu Style Tai Ji Quan.

In the Wu Style Tai Ji Quan lineage, we respect Quan You as the first generation. In the second generation were Quan You's son, Wu Jian Quan, and Quan You's senior disciple, Wang Mao Zhai. These masters led the art to other locations, thus creating the southern and northern groups of Wu Style Tai Ji Quan.

Northern Wu Style Master Wang Mao Zhai was a very famous fighter, considered the best in Beijing at the time. He became famous on the strength of his fighting skill and was widely respected in the community but totally unknown to the outside world until mayor Yuan Liang became his student. When Yang Cheng Fu opened the school to the public, he became the most prolific tai ji quan teacher in history and led the way for other public instructors of the art. He, Chen Fa Ke, Wu Jian Quan, and Wang Mao Zhai were the leading public teachers of their time.

Famous Northern Wu Style Tai Ji Quan Masters

The personal stories of the masters of the style have always been deeply entwined with the history and development of the art. Their life was typically a journey to achieve their goals in the art. For past and future generations, these masters have been and will always be remembered and respected.

The Founder, Wu Quan You

Great grandmaster Wu Quan You (1834–1902) was the founder of Wu Style Tai Ji Quan. Born in Da Xing County, he was a Manchurian and a member of the Imperial Palace guard in Beijing. He learned tai ji quan from the founder of Yang Style, Master Yang Lu Chan. Quan You's specialty was neutralization. He also studied with Yang Lu Chan's son, Yang Ban Hou. Through decades of training, he became a very well-known master who had the true skills of Yang Family tai ji quan. Based on the principles of tai ji quan, he founded his own style of the art—the Wu Style.

There are no images of Quan You, but a picture of the imperial guard shows what he must have looked like in the nineteen century, or late Qing Dynasty. Quan You was one of the very best martial artists of his time. He had the characteristics of softness in appearance and strength on the inside, and he loved to help people in their time of need. Legends have been passed down from earlier generations, telling

The imperial guard

us that Quan You had both high skills of martial ability and the true movement of martial art. He was a generous man with moral concepts melded into his skills. He never used his strength against weak people, but instead always showed kindness to others. Quan You is known to have punished those who were evil and unjust to others, and was known as a brave man who was always ready to help the needy.

One day, as the story goes, Quan You walked to the farmer's market where he saw a soldier take food from a vender and then refuse to pay. When the vender asked the soldier to pay him, the soldier started to beat the small man. Quan You came to stop the soldier, but the soldier thought Quan You looked too gentle to know how to fight, so he threw a punch and followed with a kick at Quan You. The soldier suddenly found that he himself was like a praying mantis trying to knock down a tree; he fell to the ground without Quan You having moved an inch. Quan You told the soldier that one never should use his martial skills to mistreat innocent people.

In Quan You's time martial artists often challenged each other with or without notice. Among these men, the Wu Style, due to its softness, was often mistaken as a weak martial art. One afternoon, Quan You was reading in his room when he was informed that an unknown guest had come to him. Quan You came to the courtyard to greet the man. The guest lowered his body as if to bow to Quan You, and Quan You returned the salute, but at that moment, the guest was suddenly up in the air, falling backward and landing outside the courtyard gate. All the people present were shocked by this surprise exit, but the truth was that the guest had used a martial technique known as "the steel fist" to attack Quan You's belly while pretending to bow. Quan You had in turn used the tai ji quan skills of neutralizing and redirecting power from the guest to efficiently combine defense and offense.

Quan You had three primary disciples: his son Wu Jian Quan (1870–1942), Wang Mao Zhai (1862–1940), and Guo Fen.

Master Wu Jian Quan

Master Wu Jian Quan (1870–1942), son of Quan You, modified the forms taught to him by his father. He utilized a narrower circle and created many new ways to apply the form in a practical manner. In 1924, Master Wu Jian Quan, along with his colleagues Xi Yu Sheng, Yang Shaou Hou, and Yang Cheng Fu, founded a famous martial arts school. This had an important impact on the practice of tai ji quan as the art became available to the general public for the first time.

When Wu Jian Quan first began to teach in Beijing, he taught the Yang Small Frame as handed down by his father, Quan You. This form is almost identical to the form handed down by Wang Mao Zhai.

Master Wu Jian Quan moved south to Shanghai in 1928. There he was appointed to the Board of Directors of the Shanghai Martial Arts Association. Subsequently, he became supervisor of the tai ji quan section of the famous Jing Wu Sports Association. In 1935, he established the first Wu Style Tai Ji Quan academy in Shanghai. Thus, this style has been primarily transmitted from Beijing, Shanghai, and Hong Kong.

Wu Jian Quan's daughter, Wu Ying Hua (1906–1996), and her husband, Ma Yue Liang (1901–1998), led the Shanghai Jian Quan Tai Ji Quan Society, founded in 1932 by Wu Jian Quan.

Master Wang Mao Zhai

Master Wang Mao Zhai (1862–1940) was born in Da Wu Guan Village, Yie County, in Shan Dong Province and spent his adult life in Beijing. He pursued Quan You for three years in an effort to learn tai ji quan. During this time, he reportedly learned only one posture from Quan You—"Golden Pheasant Stands On One Leg." Impressed by his sincerity and perseverance, Quan You finally taught him the rest of the Wu Style Tai Ji Quan. After twenty years of dedicated practice, Wang Mao Zhai achieved an exceptionally high level of skill in the art. When Wu Jian Quan and Yang Cheng Fu moved to southern China in 1928, Master Wang Mao Zhai continued to lead the Wu Style Beijing group, which became the biggest tai ji quan group of its time. He was the founder of the Bei Ping (Beijing) Tai Miao Tai Ji Quan Research Center, which became a gathering place for highly skilled tai ji quan practitioners. Thousands of students participated in tai ji quan practice, from the mayor of Beijing to army generals and from business people to martial arts experts. Wang Mao Zhai's high level of skill earned him a justifiably excellent reputation. The form handed down by Wang Mao Zhai is identical to Quan You's form as well as to the form Wu Jian Quan practiced in his early days.

Wang laid the foundation of the Wu Style in Beijing and influenced the entire northeast region, as well as the Shan Dong areas in northern China. The Wu Style became a strong system under Wang Mao Zhai's leadership. Masters Wang Mao Zhai and Wu Jian Quan were referred to as the Northern Wang and Southern Wu representatives of Wu Style Tai Ji Quan in China.

In 1929, the first documentary book of Wu Style Tai Ji Quan (太极功同门录, translated as *The Record of Wu Style Tai Ji Quan,* long out of print) was published by Wang Mao Zhai, Wu Jian Quan, and Guo Fen.

Master Yang Yu Ting

Wang Mao Zhai's primary disciple was Yang Yu Ting (1887–1982). He was born in Beijing and studied martial arts from the age of nine. He trained with a number of different masters and in a number of different styles, including tan tui, chang quan, xing i quan, ba gua zhang, and tai ji quan. He started to teach martial arts when he was only twenty years old and during his more than seventy years of teaching Yang trained tens of thousands of students. He studied Wu Style Tai Ji Quan under Wang Mao Zhai from 1916 to 1940. Under Master Wang Mao Zhai's instruction, Yang Yu Ting reformed the traditional long form. After Wang Mao Zhai died, Yang Yu Ting became the leader of the Wu Style Beijing group. Yang Yu Ting felt that some aspects of the old training methods were not good for practitioners, so in the 1930s he started to reform tai ji quan training. He was the first master who recognized how important it is to make training more systematic. In 1936 he standardized all the movements of Northern Wu Style Tai Ji Quan in great detail. This standardization makes it easier and more efficient for people to quickly learn the form correctly. Today this method is applied in most martial arts study groups.

Yang Yu Ting was a well-respected and active teacher in Beijing for seventy-five years. He had a superior understanding of the internal aspects of Quan You's teaching, which he acquired through studying with Wang Mao Zhao. Yang devoted his life to Chinese martial arts, especially the researching and developing of Northern Wu Style Tai Ji Quan in Beijing and the passing of that art on to many students including Wang Pei Sheng, Li Jing Wu, and Li Bing Ci. Yang actively held the vice-chairmanship of the Beijing Martial Arts Association at the time of his death at age ninety-five.

Yang Yu Ting's Northern Wu Style Tai Ji Quan postures

Yang Yu Ting's Northern Wu Style Tai Ji Quan postures

Master Wang Pei Sheng

Wang Pei Sheng (1919–2004) was born in Wu Qing County, Hebei Province. He started his martial arts training at age twelve. Having been born in 1919, Wang Pei Sheng was the youngest among the masters of the post-Qing Dynasty, pre-PRC generation. His earliest training was with Ba Gua Zhang master Ma Gui, where Wang inherited the Yin Style Ba Gua Zhang 64 Palms and Shi Ba Jie Broadsword form. One year later he was introduced to Yang Yu Ting, who became his teacher in Wu Style Tai Ji Quan. Wang quickly captured the attention of Wang Mao Zhai, patriarch at that time of Northern Wu Style Tai Ji Quan, and for years Wang received daily personal training from Wang Mao Zhai. Wang's reputation rose quickly because of his fighting ability. He began assisting Yang Yu Ting in daily tai ji quan classes at the age of fifteen. When he was eighteen, he started to teach his own classes and became the youngest of all the teachers in Beijing at the time. In 1939, he used tai ji quan techniques to beat four Japanese soldiers who, carrying guns, had followed him on his way to Tai Miao Tai Ji Quan Research Center. This became a well-known story among the people of Beijing. Wang Pei Sheng went on to succeed Yang Yu Ting as the head of the Northern Wu Style Tai Ji Quan group.

His time was that of a bridge between the old and the new. His knowledge was wide and deep, both subtle and refined, and he presided over a period of synthesizing, adopting, and creating new methods and approaches. Wang is noted for his expertise in the self-defense applications of Wu Style Tai Ji Quan. In his book *Wu Style Tai Chi Chuan* (Zhaohua Publishing House, Beijing, 1983), Wang presented the 37-posture form of Wu Style Tai Ji Quan he developed in the early 1950s. Wang Pei Sheng dedicated his life to passing on the traditional art of Northern Wu Style Tai Ji Quan to younger generations.

Master Li Bing Ci

Master Li Bing Ci was born in November 1929 in Beijing. He has practiced Chinese martial arts since he was a teenager. Li studied Wu Style Tai Ji Quan under Grandmaster Yang Yu Ting from 1946 to 1982. He also studied with well-known martial arts masters: Shi Zheng Gang, Luo Xing Wu, Shan Xiang Ling, Liu Tan Feng, in the arts of cha chuan, da bei chuan, xing yi quan, and ba gua zhang. In 1958 and 1963, Li Bing Ci won gold medals in Wu Style Tai Ji Quan, in two of the Martial Arts Grand Ceremonies and Competitions of Beijing. Li continued to study and research Northern Wu Style Tai Ji Quan and became a true master, highly respected throughout the world. In 1995, he was selected as one of the one hundred outstanding martial artists in China. Li Bing Ci is an eighth duan in Chinese national martial arts rankings. (Note: The duan system is an official Chinese government system for ranking martial arts instructors. Although the system goes to ten, to the authors' knowledge there have never been any tenth-level rankings awarded. In fact, the few ninth-level rankings awarded are considered to be more political appointments than actual grade of performance, making an eighth duan ranking the highest a working martial arts instructor can get.)

As a professional martial arts teacher, tournament judge, and researcher for more than fifty years, his life has been devoted to tai ji quan. During the early years of the cultural revolution, Li was forced to stop teaching martial arts at the sport center in the eastern district in Beijing, which he had helped to establish. But Li never stopped practicing every day at home and continued to transmit the knowledge to his student by training them in the backyard of his house. Li has taught thousands of great martial artists around the world in the traditional training methods of Wu Style Tai Ji Quan and has coached many championship winners in tai ji quan competitions in China. He is the current president of the Beijing Wu Style Tai Ji Quan Research Center.

Master Li Bing Ci and Master Men Hui Fen created the 45-posture Wu Style Tai Ji Quan official competition routine in 1988. This form has the reputation among its practitioners as a form that embraces both competition and tradition. When created, this form was based on traditional Wu Style Tai Ji Quan with a combination of movements from both the Southern and the Northern schools. This form includes all the signature postures of the later form developed by Wu Jian Quan, while preserving the main structure of the traditional Northern Wu Style routine. Li Bing Ci is one of the most respected teachers in Beijing practicing Northern Wu Style Tai Ji Quan today. At age seventy-six this year, Li may still be seen teaching tai ji quan to groups of people

in the parks, as well as in physical education centers, training professional Wu Shu teams from places other than China. Li Bing Ci is the co-author of the books *Yang Yu Ting's Tai Ji Quan* and *Wu Style Tai Ji Quan and Weapons*. (Note: Both books are available only in Chinese.)

Tina C. Zhang with master Li Bing Ci at Shi Sha Hai Sport Center, Beijing.

Characteristics of Northern Wu Style Tai Ji Quan

Perhaps the most significant aspect that distinguishes Wu Style Tai Ji Quan is its emphasis on the application of an internal approach to developing power. It emphasizes correct movements of qi through the deeper systems inside the human body (spine, internal organs, spaces in the joints, and so on) to create correct and efficient physical movements and body alignments. It is the most rigorously defined style of tai ji quan, perfect for those who require absolute precision in every movement and who enjoy the challenges such training brings as well as the benefits of practicing tai ji quan.

Traditional Chinese medicine theory is the root of tai ji quan. This is especially true for the Northern Wu Style Tai Ji Quan, which contains the soft, fluid, and gentle movements to cultivate and generate qi in the body, to balance or release the accumulated tension or blockage in the muscles, tendons, and inner organs of the body, and enhance the functioning of the body's health system. Generally, when qi, or energy, guided by the yi, or mind, helps the blood to properly circulate through the meridian channels of the entire body, physical health is achieved, and the li, or power, can then be developed by constant practice.

Movements in Wu Style Tai Ji Quan are relatively small and compact, emphasizing the manipulating of connective tissue in opening and closing the joints rather than employing the expansive postures that characterize the Yang Style. This has resulted in 324 segments of 83 postures with extreme detail in terms of direction, intent, breathing, and other internal principles.

The concentration on inner movement of this style helps to encourage an internal rather than external focus. Learning the very finely detailed movements that easily produce internal energy and strengthening the postures with a higher degree of difficulty is how Wu Style Tai Ji Quan is studied as an internal art, even in the initial stages of training.

The postures in Wu Style Tai Ji Quan are recognizable by some special appearance characteristics. The extensive opening of the space between the thumb and index finger and the usage of this "Tiger's Mouth," *hu kou,* is an excellent way to open one's palm and relax all the fingers. The Tiger's Mouth is also an important technique in martial applications for blocking, hooking, and grasping in Wu Style Tai Ji Quan.

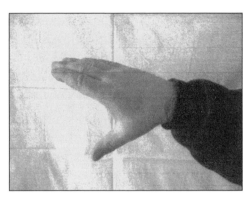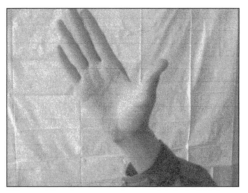

The Tiger's Mouth—opening the space between the thumb and index finger

The Ox Plow Stance features a straight back yet slanting spinal alignment—a trademark of Wu Style Tai Ji Quan. This posture allows practitioners to have a fully expanded spine and skeletal joints and transfer a maximum amount of short-range power to their hands without losing their central alignment, which is still straight from the head to foot.

Wu Jian Quan in Ox Plow stance

Yang Yu Ting in Ox Plow stance

Wu Style Tai Ji Quan's special softness of movement, comfortable expanded postures, unique footwork, straight when slanting spinal alignment (Ox Plow Stance), perfectly connected transitions between each postures, neutralization skills, and effective martial combat have gained the art many enthusiasts around the world. It is interesting to note that many Wu Style Tai Ji Quan practitioners have lived to a very advanced age.

CHAPTER 3

THE PRINCIPLES OF WU STYLE TAI JI QUAN

WHETHER A MARTIAL ART can be considered internal or external begins with the basic approach to the study of the art. Most martial arts develop from a foundation of fighting. To perfect fighting techniques, the external martial arts practitioner trains for strength and speed in fighting, learns healing techniques to recover from fighting, and practices meditation to remove hesitation and increase concentration while fighting. The internal martial arts don't concentrate on perfecting fighting techniques as their primary goal. Instead, they concentrate on building a foundation of internal energy, or qi. From this base of qi development arise the three equal pillars of fighting art, healing art, and meditation art.

Aside from an ideological foundation, the primary difference between the internal and external arts is the method of generating power. The external arts use muscular contraction to create force, in combination with cardiovascular endurance, subconscious reflex patterns, and hand-eye coordination speed. The internal arts combine manipulation of qi with full body movement, a relaxed coiling of the muscles, expansion and compression of the body's openings, a pumping rhythm of bodily fluids, an endurance that comes from diaphragmatic breathing, and muscular and emotional relaxation. While all of that is happening on the physical level, the internal practitioner applies clear, be-here-now thought and moment-to-moment decision-making that never relies on subconscious reflex patterns. Speed is often replaced in emphasis by timing and positioning. These abilities of the internal arts are attained through strict adherence to a set of principles that define a martial art as internal.

Principles of Internal Posture

Like all styles of tai ji quan, Northern Wu Style Tai Ji Quan shares the principles of the internal arts.

Stance training follows the principles of internal posture. Posture is taught from the ground up, beginning with the feet, which are kept flat on the floor, consciously feeling the pressure on the soles and maintaining an even weight distribution on the balls of the feet, and down the sides and across the heels. The feet are spaced hip-width apart to shoulder-width apart.

The knees are never locked but always have a slight bend. They must always be aligned above the feet, never extending beyond the toes. This alignment allows the knees to transfer the body weight from the hips to the feet. Other alignments cause the knees to bear the body's weight, which often leads to knee injuries.

The point in the center of the crotch, known in English as the perineum and in Chinese as the *hui yin*, is the starting and connecting point to *ren mai* and *du mai*, the meridian channels that together form the microcosmic orbit that connects the torso and head. The hui yin, or perineum, is also the transfer point from the torso to the legs for many nerves, blood vessels, and other energy channels. When the perineum is folded upon itself and closed, energy flow to and from the legs is severely limited.

The pelvis is tucked forward, thereby flattening the sacrum, stretching the lumbar spine, and causing the tail bone to feel as if it is pointed at the floor. The practitioner then sinks down and back as if preparing to sit on a chair. This aligns the buttocks over the heals while folding the inguinal crease, where the legs attach to the torso. The inguinal crease is a major movement section of the pelvic area, which in Chinese is known as the *kua*. The kua, or pelvic area, which includes the sacrum where the spine and hips join and the big ball-and-socket joints of the hips, functions as the body's biggest joint and connects the upper and lower halves of the body. In Northern Wu Style Tai Ji Quan, all movements originate from this kua area, making this the most important part of the body for practitioners. Therefore, much effort and attention is put into the opening, flexibility, relaxation, and strengthening of this area. The strong and healthy kua of the Northern Wu Style practitioner becomes both a source of martial power and a central point for the strengthening of general health.

The spine is lifted and the shoulders are dropped. The shoulder blades are spread apart, which rounds and widens the chest and opens the armpits. The center of the armpits must stay open to facilitate energy flow between the torso and the arms, just as the opening of the perineum does for the flow of energy between the torso and the legs.

The muscles of the chest and abdomen are completely relaxed and dropped. The sides of the body, between the top of the hip and the bottom of the ribs, are lifted equally to open the solar plexus and keep pressure off the diaphragm.

The junction of the spine and the skull is kept flat, while the chin and jaw line are held parallel to the floor. The chin neither juts forward nor tucks back into the neck.

The practitioner lifts from the crown of the skull, while simultaneously sitting into the crease of the hips, thereby keeping a slight but constant stretch on the spine.

Principles of Breathing

Breathing should be done through the nose with the tip of the tongue at the roof of the mouth just behind the teeth. All breathing is powered by movement of the diaphragm wall instead of the muscles between the ribs. Externally, this creates the feeling of breathing with the low waist instead of breathing with the upper chest. Internally, the diaphragm wall, which is located between the chest and abdominal cavities, is lowered and raised, instead of contracting and relaxing intercostal muscles in the rib cage. The diaphragm lowers to make room for the opening at the bottom of the lungs. This is the only method of breathing to efficiently oxygenate the body; it is the breathing method used by horn players and opera singers. Diaphragmatic breathing also lowers a fighter's center of gravity, rooting the person into the floor so that it is much more difficult to be knocked down.

This type of breathing is often called belly breathing, or dan tian breathing, but it is very important to use the entire waist, including the sides and the low back, and not just the belly in front. The lungs are toward the back of the chest cavity, so it is important to lower the back of the diaphragm wall. The pumping of the low waist and the stillness of the lowered upper chest area limits the activity in a person's emotional center to help the practitioner stay relaxed and keep a clear head.

Principles of Vision and Mind-Set

Development of relaxed eyesight is a special training method of tai ji quan. The concept is to simply let images come into the eyes and stop projecting vision out to the images. This results in a wide-angle vision that might at first be slightly soft-focus. It is difficult to stop outward projection of vision, but when this is accomplished, the practitioner has a much larger range of vision and perception. Relaxed vision also relieves eye strain.

Free-flowing thought is the base of the mind-set principle. The tai ji quan practitioner simply fights no thoughts out of his or her mind, and holds no thoughts in. Thoughts flow through the mind freely while being gently focused on the here and now and avoiding thoughts of the past, the future, or fantasy. This mind-set is necessary for the martial applications of tai ji quan, while also promoting mental and emotional health and creating the foundations for a practice of Taoist meditation.

Traditionally, the principles of posture, breathing, vision, and mind-set are practiced, at first, while holding the postures of the tai ji quan form. Later, with practice and familiarity, the principles are applied to the form as a whole movement and to the fighting practices themselves.

Principles of Movement

These principles disavow the movement of individual body parts. The classic way of expressing the first principle, unity of movement, is "One part moves, all parts move! One part stops, all parts stop!" This well-known phrase means that all parts of each movement must reach the change point at the same time, so that all parts can change together. One of the easiest methods of learning this principle is with the practice of the posture "Cloud Hands," in which one shifts weight, twists the torso, and circles both hands simultaneously. The unity of movement principle must be applied in all movement in order to apply the second principle, the continuity of flow: When all the parts of a movement reach the change point at the same time, the flow of movement can remain unbroken throughout the change. Unity of movement is also learned by stopping at the change point to be sure that each part of the movement has reached its change point at the same time. Once unity of movement is achieved, the practitioner does not need to stop at the change points to check correctness, but rather begins to flow through the change points and create an unbroken flow of physical movement. This unbroken flow of physical movement helps to regulate the circulation of blood in the body. This same unbroken flow of movement is the secret behind much of the timing and positioning in internal martial arts.

The unbroken flow of physical movement must be matched with the unbroken flow of breath and the unbroken flow of thought to create the potential for an unbroken flow of energy. Energy flow is learned through many methods. One of the more common methods is through slow repetitions of form practice. Many slow repetitions are necessary. Without a lot of energy practice, it is difficult to feel the flow of energy. When the energy movement is clearly felt, the practitioner begins to let the energy movement lead the physical movement. Eventually, the energy leads the body through all movements of exercise, form, and fighting. When the unbroken flow of energy matches the unbroken flow of movement, breath, and thought, the complete unity of movement principle has been achieved.

Principle of Compression and Expansion

There are three parts to each compression and expansion movement: two booster parts and the main act. The auxiliary parts are the drop through the hip crease and the accordion action of the dan tian, or lower belly. The main act is the actual compression and expansion of the joints of the skeleton.

Hip crease squats develop the ability to drop into the crease (the line where the legs join the body), without bending the knees or leaning forward. This small movement requires stretching the iliopsoas muscle group, which connects the spine to the hip and thigh (the muscle group is made up of the psoas major, attaching the spine to the femur, and the iliacus, attaching the hip to the femur). Like most stretching, only very small movement is possible or recommended at first. As the hips drop, the muscles of the lower belly relax completely, almost jellifying and folding in on themselves. As the hips rise, the lower belly fills with energy and air and rounds out. At no time during the belly accordion action do the muscles of the belly tense. The hip crease squats and the belly accordion action help the expanding and compressing of the joints.

The hip dropping and the belly folding in help all the places of the body where two or more bones come together to pull at their respective junctures. As the hips rise and belly fills out, all of the bones push apart. This expansion stretches the ligaments, which connect bone to bone, and the membrane that encapsulates the joint. When it is stretched, this membrane secretes synovial fluid to lubricate the joint. The early practice of compression and expansion serves to open and lubricate all the joints that were closed, tight, and lacking fluid. This is how internal martial arts and tai ji quan helps prevent joint disease and heal joint injuries. The hip crease squat also pumps the lymph nodes in that area, helping to increase the flow of lymphatic fluid to strengthen the immune system.

When the joints are open and healthy, the internal martial artist begins to learn how to use compression and expansion movements to create internal hydraulic power for short-range action. This power is created by first compressing all the joints in a line extending all the way to a foot, or both feet. For instance, one might start the line of compression from a fist, up that arm, through the shoulder, down the spine, and through the same side of the hip, down the leg, and into the foot. Then, once all the joints are compressed together, and the target is open and in range, all of the joints in the line are expanded or opened up simultaneously, causing the fist to thrust forward and strike the target. The distance that the fist travels in its thrust forward is equal to the sum of all the joints opening. Even though each joint might open up only a fraction of a centimeter, the sum of all these joints opening, extending from the joints in the foot, up the leg, through the hip, up the spine, out the shoulder, through the arm, wrist, and finally propelling the fist forward, is surprising large. This internal hydraulic compression power is most effective for short-range actions and can be used in conjunction with or in place of a straightening of the joints, a shifting of the weight, and/or qi discharge.

Coiling the muscles inward toward the center of the body with each compression and away from the center of the body with each expansion gives added power to the movement. This coiling action also increases the circulation of blood to the muscles and the flow of lymphatic fluid.

In Northern Wu Style Tai Ji Quan, each movement contains a compression and expansion aspect to train the power of discharge. The compression and expansion movement also opens up the large and small joints in the human body, promoting skeletal health.

Principle of Lengthening

The ability to maintain the chang, or continuous lengthening, outward from one's center in movements of flexion and compression is the paradoxical aspect of this principle. The lengthening principle is founded on the belief that the process of closing in toward one's center is a normal result of aging. A baby's body is open and relaxed with long tissues and open cavities. The adult body is more upright, but conspicuously tightened into the center, with the spine often curved unnaturally forward. The lengthening principle supports continuous, conscious lengthening of the body's tissues, joints, and cavities as an anti-aging practice.

Maintaining the lengthening principle during actions of extension and expansion is normal and happens quite naturally. Lengthening during actions of flexion and compression, however, requires a subtle feeling of continuously opening away from the center of the body, even as certain body parts flex and compress inward. The continuous coiling of the muscle tissues must be maintained to achieve this subtle feeling. It's a matter of stretching inward during closing movements, rather than collapsing inward.

The lengthening principle is difficult to maintain, but it is not difficult to spot an internal martial arts form that does not maintain this principle. The form appears to be limp, powerless, and lifeless. Maintaining a proper lengthening principle gives internal movements grace and power, while helping to improve the health and longevity of the practitioner. In both Northern Wu Style empty-hand and sword forms there are many postures and movements designed to facilitate the lengthening principle.

Harmony of Opposites

The harmony of opposites is one of the foundation principles of Chinese civilization, including the philosophy of Taoism and internal boxing. The harmony of opposites principle is symbolized by the yin-yang, or tai ji, design.

The internal boxing styles manifest the principle of harmony of yin and yang in various methods. Tai ji quan is named for the principle and softly applies its balance of yin and yang with its empty and full movements. As a soft art, tai ji quan yields and moves with an oncoming force until it can find a place of no resistance to apply its own force. The change from yielding to advancing is tai ji quan's trademark harmonious yin-to-yang movement. The change from light to heavy and empty to full are the yin-yang balance in the solo form of tai ji quan.

CHAPTER 4

THE HAND POSITIONS AND STANCES OF NORTHERN WU STYLE TAI JI QUAN

LEARNING AND PRACTICING THE BASIC HAND POSITIONS and basic stances is a good way to obtain initial knowledge of this tai ji quan style. One can also practice the basic stances as a warm-up before doing the whole form or attempting tai ji quan postures.

The Basic Hand Positions

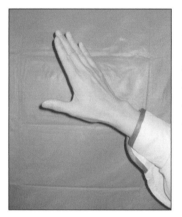

In the open-hand position, the thumb is separated from the fingers to make the hu kou, or Tiger's Mouth. The fingers should be straight but naturally relaxed and the palm is open and flat. A major acupuncture point, which is stimulated by this position, lies between the thumb and the index finger and about one inch in from the edge of the hand.

Open hand

In the whip, or hooked-hand position, the four fingers are curved toward the thumb, and all five finger tips touch each other. The wrist bends and lifts upward.

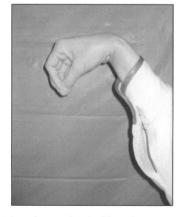

The whip, or hooked hand position

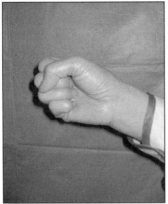

In the tai ji fist position, the thumb is folded over the rest of fingers, which are gently folded into the palm. The muscles of the hand and fingers remain relaxed so that the fist can give inward on impact.

The tai ji fist position

The Basic Stances

Pay attention to a few position reminders when doing tai ji quan stances: knees should be soft (not locked); feet flat on the ground; weight evenly balanced between the two feet, unless stated otherwise as "60%–40%" (or other) distributed or 100% on one leg for the empty stances; knee aligned over the foot and never extending beyond the toe.

Front stance

Horse stance

Cross stance   Crouching stance

Empty stance   Empty stance (toes up on the   Crane stance
                           empty leg)

Figure eight stance   Resting stance

CHAPTER 5

THE CLASSICAL FORM AND APPLICATIONS

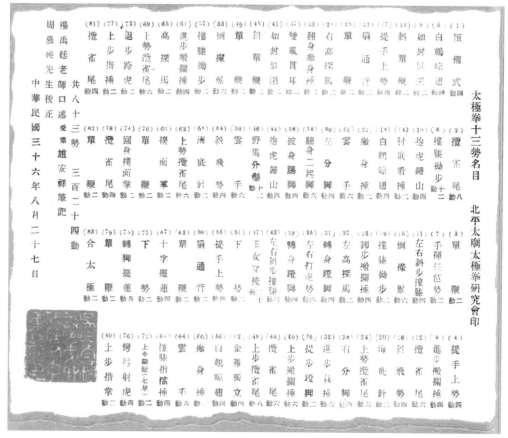

The names and order of the Classical Wu Style Tai Ji Quan postures

THIS CHART OF THE 83 POSTURES and 324 movements of the Wu Style Tai Ji Quan form (Quan You's form) was documented by Yang Yu Ting at Beijing Tai Miao Tai Ji Quan Research Center in 1947.

The traditional form is known as the "Tai Ji Quan Thirteen Postures." The "thirteen postures" refers to the eight directions and the five elements.

Here are the names and sequence of the 83 postures of the Classical Northern Wu Style Tai Ji Quan form:

1. Opening 预备势
2. Grasp Sparrow's Tail 揽雀尾
3. Oblique Single Whip 单鞭
4. Lift Hands Upward 提手上势
5. White Crane Displays Its Wings 白鹤亮翅
6. Brush Knee Twist Step 搂膝拗步
7. Play the Pipa 手挥琵琶
8. Advance, Deflect, Parry, and Punch 进步搬拦捶
9. Apparent Closing 如封似闭
10. Embrace the Tiger, Return to Mountain 抱虎归山
11. Brush Knee Twist Step 左右搂膝拗步
12. Grasp Sparrow's Tail 揽雀尾
13. Oblique Single Whip 斜单鞭
14. Observe Fist Under Elbow 肘底捶
15. Step Backward, Repulse the Monkey 倒撵猴
16. Fly Obliquely 斜飞势
17. Lift Hands Upward 提手上势
18. White Crane Displays Its Wings 白鹤亮翅
19. Brush Knee Twist Step 搂膝拗步
20. Needle At the Sea Bottom 海底针
21. Fan through the Back 扇通背
22. Turn Body and Fist Strike 撇身捶
23. Deflect, Parry, and Punch搬拦捶
24. Step Forward and Grasp Sparrow's Tail 上步拦雀尾
25. Single Whip 单鞭
26. Cloud Hands 云手
27. Left High Pat the Horse 左高探马
28. Right Toe Kick 右分脚
29. Right High Pat the Horse 右高探马
30. Left Toe Kick 左高探马

31. Turn Body, Kick with Heel 转身蹬脚
32. Advance and Punch Low 进步栽捶
33. Turn Body and Fist Strike 翻身撇身捶
34. Turn Body, Second Kick with Heel 翻身二起脚
35. Strike the Tiger 左右打虎势
36. Step and Heel Kick 提步蹬脚
37. Double Wind to the Ears 双峰贯耳
38. Crouch and Kick 披身踢脚
39. Turn and Kick 转身蹬脚
40. Advance, Deflect, Parry, and Punch 进步搬拦捶
41. Apparent Closing 如封似闭
42. Embrace the Tiger, Return to Mountain 抱虎归山
43. Brush Knee Twist Step 搂膝拗步
44. Grasp Sparrow's Tail 拦雀尾
45. Oblique Single Whip 斜单鞭
46. Part the Wild Horse's Mane 野马分鬃
47. Fair Lady Works the Shuttle 玉女穿梭
48. Advance, Grasp Sparrow's Tail 上步拦雀尾
49. Single Whip 单鞭
50. Cloud Hands 云手
51. Snake Creeps Down 下势
52. Golden Cock Stands on One Leg 金鸡独立
53. Step Backward, Repulse the Monkey 倒撵猴
54. Fly Obliquely 斜飞势
55. Lift Hands Upward 提手上势
56. White Crane Displays Its Wings 白鹤亮翅
57. Brush Knee Twist Step 搂膝拗步
58. Needle At the Sea Bottom 海底针
59. Fan through the Back 扇通背
60. Turn Body and Fist Strike 撇身捶
61. Advance, Deflect, Parry, and Punch 进步搬拦捶
62. Step Forward and Grasp Sparrow's Tail 上势拦雀尾

63. Single Whip 单鞭
64. Cloud Hands 云手
65. High Pat the Horse 高探马
66. Palm Strike 扑面掌
67. Cross Hands, Sweep Lotus 十字摆莲
68. Brush Knee, Punch Toward Groin 搂膝指裆捶
69. Step Forward, Grasp Sparrow's Tail 上势拦雀尾
70. Single Whip 单鞭
71. Snake Creeps Down 下势
72. Step Forward to Seven Stars 上步七星
73. Retreat, Astride the Tiger 退步跨虎
74. Turn Body and Palm Strike to the Face 回身扑面掌
75. Turn Body, Sweep Lotus 转身摆莲
76. Draw the Bow and Shoot the Tiger 弯弓射虎
77. Step Forward and Fist Strike 上步措捶
78. Step Forward and Grasp Sparrow's Tail 拦雀尾
79. Single Whip 单鞭
80. Step Forward and Palm Strike 上步措掌
81. Grasp Sparrow's Tail 拦雀尾
82. Single Whip 单鞭
83. Closing 合太极

The names of the postures in tai ji quan are a part of Chinese culture and have different connotations. They have been beautifully named to describe the manner in which movements should be physically practiced, such as the ways of nature like "Wave Hands Like Clouds," or animal movements like" White Crane Displays Its Wings." Each name is a tool to help the practitioner to remember the movement or posture as well as to discover the martial application of that posture or movement.

In ancient China, tai ji quan masters taught their students to orally pass down the names of the postures of tai ji quan to their disciples. The chart of the names of the postures of Wu Style Tai Ji Quan at the beginning of this chapter was given as an oral account by Master Yang Yu Ting and written down by Zhao An Xiang and Zhou Mu Chun. It was named "Tai Ji Quan Thirteen Postures," or *Taiji Shi San Shi* in Chinese. That was a another way that tai ji quan, in general, was referred to at that time. This name related to Wu Style Tai Ji Quan's theory, in which the eight directions represent the eight tai ji quan techniques of *peng, lu, ji, an, cai, lie, zhou, kao* and the five elements of *jin, mu, shui, huo, tu,* which when added to the eight directions complete the number thirteen.

The Classical Northern Wu Style Tai Ji Quan Form

The Northern Wu Style Tai Ji Quan form is performed in eight different directions. We will indicate them as we move through the postures.

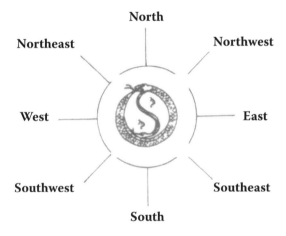

1: Opening

Begin with a natural standing posture, looking forward with a level gaze and facing the South. Relax the entire body and breathe slowly and evenly (Figure 5-1).

Figure 5-1

Pick up your left foot, stepping to the left about shoulder width; weight is gradually transferred from the right to the center with the knees slightly bent and the whole feet touching the ground. Lower your center of gravity and sink the qi to the dan tian area. Also keep the spine straight, shoulders relaxed, and the crown of the head tilted upward (Figure 5-2).

Figure 5-2 *Figure 5-3* *Figure 5-4*

Lift both arms and hands to your front with palms facing each other, and then gradually turn the palms to face downward when the arms are shoulder height. Hands are shoulder width. Lower the arms and hands downward together to both sides of the kua, or pelvic area, sinking the center of gravity even farther downward (Figures 5-3 and 5-4).

2: Grasp Sparrow's Tail

Step forward, first with the left foot, heels touching the floor first. Raise both hands together from the sides to the center front. The left hand coils so the palm faces toward you; the right hand touches the left wrist, palm facing outward (Figure 5-5). Shift the weight forward and push the hands forward a bit (Figure 5-6). Then turn the left heel to the left (outward) and simultaneously turn the body and the right foot (on toe) to the right without the weight shifting, as the right hand travels over the left hand until the palm faces upward. Then step the right foot in front, heel first, to form a front stance. You are now facing the West (Figures 5-7 and 5-8). Continue extending the body forward into the front stance and turn the right hand to face downward, and left hand upward (Figure 5-9).

Figure 5-5 Figure 5-6 Figure 5-7

Figure 5-8 Figure 5-9 Figure 5-10

Shift the weight onto the left leg and pull back both hands to the side of the right thigh with the right heel on the ground (Figure 5-10). Then turn the right hand and left hand palm up. Send the hands forward while coming into a front stance and then the hands continue to travel horizontally to the right side of the body, while the weight shifts to the left leg and the right foot points the toes up (Figures 5-11 and 5-12). Bend the right elbow and turn the left palm face upward and the right palm facing forward, pushing forward as well and turning on the right heel, making the body face the front with the weight on this leg. You are now facing the South again (Figure 5-13).

Figure 5-11   Figure 5-12   Figure 5-13

3: Oblique Single Whip

Form the right hand into a hook by moving it to the right a little and then bending the wrist and curving the fingers together until the thumb touches all the finger tips at the same time. Lower your center of gravity, which is also called "sinking down the kua" (Figure 5-14). Step with the left leg to the left side at a 45-degree angle, with toes touching the floor first. Shift the body weight toward the left until the weight is centered in a horse stance and the left palm has moved from the left to the right across the chest, with the palm coiling from facing inward to outward. The eyes follow the left hand's movement, to look toward the Southeast (Figure 5-15).

Figure 5-14   Figure 5-15

4: Lift Hands Upward

Shift the weight to face South again, with a pivot of the left heel and with both hands coming up from the sides to the front of the chest, with the right palm inward and the left palm on the right wrist facing outward (Figure 5-16). Then shift the weight forward into a deep right front stance (Figure 5-17).

Figure 5-16   *Figure 5-17*

The right hand becomes a hooked hand, lifting upward gradually and changing to palm forward when it gets above the head. The left hand drops to be even with the dan tian. At the same time, the left foot steps forward to be parallel with the right foot, weight evenly distributed to both feet. Expand the whole body upward while keeping the feet rooted, looking upward without bending the neck backward and keeping the spine straight (Figures 5-18 and 5-19).

Figure 5-18   *Figure 5-19*

5: White Crane Displays Its Wings

Bend the body downward without curling the spine until the entire back is parallel to the ground, extending the left hand to the center front as near to the ground as possible (Figure 5-20). Then turn to the left while holding this posture, turning the left palm outward (Figure 5-21), and continue to lift upward and back into the standing posture. Then bend the elbows and lower the arms with the palms coiling inward until the palms face you with the body sinking downward (Figures 5-22, 5-23, and 5-24).

Figure 5-20   Figure 5-21   Figure 5-22

Figure 5-23   Figure 5-24   Figure 5-25

6: Brush Knee Twist Step

Continuing from the last posture, with the palms facing you, coil the left hand downward with the palm facing down, and lift the right hand up to the height of the right ear, palm facing the ear. Simultaneously shift the weight onto the right leg while opening the pelvic area (Figure 5-25) and stepping out to the left, first touching the ground with the heel. You are facing the East.

Shift the weight while bending the left leg to form a left front stance. At the same time, the left hand, following the turning of the body, passes before the left knee to the side of the left thigh, palm facing down. The right hand pushes forward (Figure 5-26). Shifting the weight onto the right leg, pull the right hand backward, and raise the left hand upward and forward, ending with palm up, while the right hand ends with palm down (Figure 5-27).

Figure 5-26   *Figure 5-27*   *Figure 5-28*

Repeat the movement in the paragraph above, to the left front stance (Figures 5-28 and 5-29). Then push downward with your right palm (Figure 5-30). Keep the weight on the left leg and straighten the spine into a further slanting forward position, pulling the right leg next to the left ankle without putting weight on the ground (an "empty stance"). At the same time, raise the left hand to the left ear (Figure 5-31).

Push forward with the left hand, while the right hand travels back to the right thigh (Figure 5-32). All these movements are simultaneous and fluidlike, ending in a right front stance. Push down the left palm (Figure 5-33) and repeat the left "Brush Knee Twist Step" movements, finishing with a left front stance (Figures 5-34 and 5-35).

Figure 5-29

Figure 5-30

Figure 5-31

Figure 5-32

Figure 5-33

Figure 5-34

Figure 5-35

Figure 5-36

Figure 5-37

7: Play the Pipa

Shift the weight to the right leg while the left hand moves forward with the palm up and the right hand moves backward with the palm down (Figure 5-36). Lower the center of gravity, turn the left palm to face downward and the right palm to face upward, and bring both of them to the front of the right kua (Figure 5-37).

Shift the weight forward, moving both hands forward to the left front side while stepping into a left front stance (Figure 5-38). Step forward with the right foot into a natural stance while coiling (turning) both palms; finish with the left palm facing up at the left front of the body and the right palm at the right side of waist (Figure 5-39).

Figure 5-38   *Figure 5-39*

8: Advance, Deflect, Parry, and Punch

Bring the left hand above the right hand, palms facing each other. While lowering the center of gravity, the waist and palms make a tiny circle (Figure 5-40). Step forward with the left into a front stance, the arms traveling to the left front. Then shift the weight to the right leg as the hands come down to the side of the left thigh (Figures 5-41 and 5-42). Coil the left palm straight forward and change the right palm into a fist at the right waist, with weight on the right leg and the left toe up (Figure 5-43). Shift the weight forward to a left front stance and punch with the right fist; rest the left hand on the right forearm (Figure 5-44).

Figure 5-40

Figure 5-41

Figure 5-42

Figure 5-43

Figure 5-44

9: Apparent Closing

The left palm moves under the right elbow (Figure 5-45). Loosen the right fist as the left hand goes forward to meet the right hand, and turn both palms facing toward you. Then shift the weight backward while pulling the palms close to the front of your shoulders (Figure 5-46). Turn the palms facing outward and push forward while shifting the weight forward on the left (Figure 5-47).

Figure 5-45   Figure 5-46   Figure 5-47

10: Embrace the Tiger, Return to Mountain

Push downward with both palms (Figure 5-48). Pivot the right heel inward first and the left heel outward, and then shift the weight to the right foot and turn to face the South with both arms opening simultaneously, palms facing down (Figure 5-49). Your body faces South, while your gaze is toward the Southwest.

Figure 5-48   Figure 5-49

The left foot comes forward to a shoulder-width stance, turning both palms up. Lift the arms above the head and cross the wrists; expand all the joints throughout the body (Figure 5-50). Then compress all the joints while lowering the center of gravity and dropping the crossed arms down to chest level (Figure 5-51).

Figure 5-50　　　　　　　　　　　　　　　　　　　　　　　　　*Figure 5-51*

11: Brush Knee Twist Step

The left foot steps forward with no weight, while lifting the right hand up to the right ear and lowering the left hand (Figure 5-52). Then shift the weight to form a left front stance, while the left hand passes around the left knee to the left thigh and the right hand pushes forward (Figure 5-53). Pivot the left heel outward while the body turns to the right, to a left empty stance, while the left hand comes up to the left ear and the right hand travels down in front of the dan tian area. Your body is facing Southwest and attention is toward the Northwest (Figure 5-54).

Figure 5-52　　　　　　　　*Figure 5-53*　　　　　　　　*Figure 5-54*

The right hand moves around the right knee to the side of the right thigh, and the left hand pushes forward with a right front stance (Figure 5-55). The left palm turns upward and the right palm faces down and passes over the left arm, as you expand both arms forward (Figure 5-56). You finish facing West.

Figure 5-55

Figure 5-56

12: Grasp Sparrow's Tail

This posture has movements identical to posture 2, but facing Southwest.

13: Oblique Single Whip

Identical to posture 3, but your body faces Southwest (Figure 5-57).

Figure 5-57

14: Observe Fist under the Elbow

After completing the Single Whip, pivot the left heel outward and turn the body to face the East while opening both arms. Reach the left hand forward and the right hand backward, both palms facing down (Figure 5-58). Swing the front hand backward and the rear hand forward. Gradually change both palms to hooked hands. Shift the weight to the right leg and step into an empty stance with the right fist under the left elbow (Figure 5-59).

Figure 5-58   *Figure 5-59*

15: Step Backward, Repulse the Monkey

Both fists become palms (Figure 5-60). Simultaneously, pulling the left palm near the left ear, lift the left knee up, while the right palm travels to the front and faces down (Figure 5-61).

The left foot reaches backward and the left hand pushes forward, while the right hand moves to the right thigh, palm facing down. Weight remains on the right leg (Figure 5-62). Shift the weight to the left leg while pulling the right palm near the right ear (Figure 5-63). Lift the right knee up as the left palm travels to the front with the palm turning to face up alongside the right foot (Figure 5-64).

The right foot reaches backward and the right hand pushes forward, while the left hand moves to the left thigh, palm facing down. Weight remains on the left leg (Figure 5-65). Shift the weight to the right leg while pulling the left palm near the left ear (Figure 5-66). Lift the left knee as the right palm travels to the front with the palm facing down (Figure 5-67). The left foot reaches backward and the left hand pushes forward, while the right hand moves to the right thigh, palm facing down. Weight remains on right leg (Figure 5-68).

These stepping-backward-while-pushing-forward movements are repeated three times in this Repulse the Monkey posture. You will finish with your weight on the right leg, pushing forward with the left hand, and facing West.

Figure 5-60

Figure 5-61

Figure 5-62

Figure 5-63

Figure 5-64

Figure 5-65

Figure 5-66   Figure 5-67   Figure 5-68

16: Fly Obliquely

Pick up the left foot and move it close to the right foot without shifting weight. Move the right hand upward to the front of left shoulder while the left hand goes downward to the right pelvic area (Figure 5-69). The left foot steps out to the left front, to a horse stance, and both hands travel to opposite directions, meeting and pausing in the center with palms facing each other (Figure 5-70). Shift more weight to the left side to form a left front stance while the hands continue to travel in different directions (Figure 5-71).

Figure 5-69   Figure 5-70   Figure 5-71

Pay special attention in doing these movements: When you move into the front stance, you are shifting the weight from one side to the other after first forming a horse stance (when you transfer the weight and it is equal in both legs, between the previous stance and the front stance). During the movement, compress all the joints in the body, then continue to shift more weight to one side and expand all the joints to form the front stance.

17: Lift Hands Upward

This is identical with posture 4.

18: White Crane Displays Its Wings

This is identical with posture 5.

19: Brush Knee Twist Step

This is identical with the posture 6.

20: Needle At the Sea Bottom

from the left front stance, facing East, shift the weight to the right leg, and turn the right palm to face to the left (Figure 5-72). The left foot steps back to an empty stance, close to the right foot. Rotate both arms in a small circle vertically, ending with the left palm close to the right ear and the right palm pointing downward at the center line. You are bending the knees and lowering the center of gravity as much as you can (Figure 5-73).

Figure 5-72   *Figure 5-73*

21: Fan through the Back

The left foot steps forward with the heel touching the ground while straightening the back (Figure 5-74). The left heel pivots inward and the ball of the right foot pivots outward to form a horse stance, facing the South. Both arms are open, with palms facing forward and the right hand raised (Figure 5-75).

Figure 5-74

Figure 5-75

22: Turn Body and Fist Strike

The left foot pivots inward and right foot draws inward, to an empty stance, while lifting both hands to the level of the forehead with the left palm "covering" the right fist (Figure 5-76). The right foot steps forward to a front stance while punching downward to the Northwest with both hands still together (Figure 5-77). The hands pull backward to the side of the right thigh (Figure 5-78).

Figure 5-76

Figure 5-77

Figure 5-78

23: Deflect, Parry, and Punch

As weight shifts to the left, with the right leg extended, the hands move forward to the front, with the left hand still covering the right fist (Figure 5-79). The right foot steps backward and weight shifts onto it, while the hands pull backward to the side of the left thigh (Figure 5-80). Pull the right fist into a chamber at the waist and extend the left hand forward with the palm facing sideways, while lowering the center of gravity (Figure 5-81). Shift the weight forward into a left front stance and punch through with the right hand; rest the left hand on the right forearm (Figure 5-82).

Figure 5-79

Figure 5-80

Figure 5-81

Figure 5-82

24: Step Forward and Grasp Sparrow's Tail

Step forward with the right foot while keeping the weight back on the left foot in an empty stance. Turn the right fist face up, resting the left palm on the right wrist area (Figure 5-83). Extend the fist forward while shifting the weight to the right foot in a front stance. Gradually turn the fist to face down, and then open it so that the palm is facing down; at the same time, turn the left palm over to face up (Figures 5-84 and 5-85).

Figure 5-83   *Figure 5-84*   *Figure 5-85*

Shift the weight backward to the left foot, with the right foot toe up, while pulling both hands to the side of the right thigh (Figure 5-86). Rotate the hands to the dan tian area, turning over both palms so that the right palm is facing up and the left palm facing down. Continue moving the rotated hands forward, shifting the weight forward to the right foot (Figure 5-87). Keep the hands in position and shift the weight backward to the left foot again, while the right foot is on the heel. Continue to circle the hands horizontally, until the right hand is facing North, palm up (Figure 5-88). Bend at both elbows so the forearms turn over, as you turn on the right heel to face the South, and shift the weight toward the right leg. Push the right palm forward, facing the South (Figure 5-89).

Figure 5-86   *Figure 5-87*   *Figure 5-88*

Figure 5-89

25: Single Whip

The right hand forms a whip hand and the left foot steps outward to the left with the ball of the foot touching the ground first (Figure 5-90). The left hand travels to the left and the palm coils gradually, facing outward at the end. The eyes are looking at the left hand and beyond (Figure 5-91).

Figure 5-90

Figure 5-91

26: Cloud Hands

The whip hand changes to an open hand, palm down, while shifting the body weight toward the right side first (Figure 5-92). Immediately the left hand circles across the dan tian area and upward while the right palm circles downward and across the dan tian area and upward to the left side, while the right foot steps close to the left foot (Figure 5-93). The center of gravity rises slightly when the feet are in their closest position (Figure 5-94). Then sink the center of gravity as the upper body turns slightly to the right side, using the kua, or pelvic area, to turn the body; at the same time, the right hand circles upward and outward from the shoulder, while the left hand circles downward and across to the right side. During these movements, the eyes follow the direction of the leading hand, which is advancing the motion and slightly higher than the other one (Figure 5-95). Repeat the Cloud Hands set of movements one more time, and close with a Single Whip, with the body facing South (Figure 5-96).

Figure 5-92   Figure 5-93   Figure 5-94

Figure 5-95   Figure 5-96

27: Left High Pat the Horse

Pivot the right toe inward and shift the weight onto the right foot, pulling the left foot toward the right to form an empty stance, facing the East. Change the whip hand to a palm hand and draw it upward and closer to the head, while turning the left hand so the palm faces up (Figure 5-97). Then rotate the arms and palms so they are facing each other in front of the body, with right palm above left palm (Figure 5-98).

Figure 5-97

Figure 5-98

28: Right Toe Kick

The left foot steps forward into a front stance and the right palm travels outward and facing down; the left hand moves beneath the right elbow, palm facing up (Figure 5-99). The right hand travels downward to the left thigh, and the left hand is in front of the right shoulder, the eyes follow the movement of the right hand (Figure 5-100).

Shift the weight onto the left leg, moving the right foot close to the left foot. Lift the right knee to form a crane stance, while both hands coil and lift upward with the hands crossing each other, palms facing out above the head (Figure 5-101). Split the arms with the right in front at a 30-degree angle and the left at the back, and kick with the right toe to form a parallel 30-degree angle (Figure 5-102).

Figure 5-99

Figure 5-100

| Figure 5-101 | Figure 5-102 | Figure 5-103 |

29: Right High Pat the Horse

After the kick, return through the crane stance (bending the leg so the foot points downward toward the left leg), and then step the right foot forward into a front stance. Bring both palms in front with the palms facing each other. The left palm cuts over the right palm, circling horizontally to the left, while the right palm moves to the right in a small horizontal circle (Figure 5-103). Attention is to the left.

30: Left Toe Kick

These movements are the same as the movements in posture 28, but in the opposite direction (Figures 5-104, 5-105, and 5-106). The body continues to face the East.

| Figure 5-104 | Figure 5-105 | Figure 5-106 |

31: Turn Body, Kick with Heel

After the kick, bring the left foot toward the standing leg, for a crane stance, while bringing both hands in to the chest and changing them to fists crossed in front of the chest (Figure 5-107). The right heel pivots to change the body direction to face the West (Figure 5-108). Open the fists to palms and separate them while the left foot kicks, the heel forward (Figure 5-109). The entire movement in this posture is done while standing in a right-leg crane stance. The pivot should be done in a single movement, if possible.

Figure 5-107   *Figure 5-108*   *Figure 5-109*

32: Advance and Punch Low

Bring the leg down through a crane stance and step forward with the heel touching the ground first. The right hand is at the side of the right ear and the left palm faces down in front of the dan tian (Figure 5-110). Shift the weight to the left foot to form a front stance as the right palm pushes forward and the left hand circles around to the left thigh, palm down (Figure 5-111). Rotate the hands, the left hand goeing upward close to the left ear, and the right hand pushing downward; at the same time, pick up the right foot and move it forward to just in front of the left foot (Figure 5-112). The right foot steps forward into a front stance with left palm pushing forward as the right palm moves to the right thigh (Figure 5-113). Repeat the movements by picking up the back foot and moving it forward, while rotating the hands (Figure 5-114) to the right ear and the dan tian. Then form a left front stance with the right fist punching low and the left palm on the forearm near the right wrist (Figure 5-115).

Figure 5-110

Figure 5-111

Figure 5-112

Figure 5-113

Figure 5-114

Figure 5-115

33: Turn Body and Fist Strike

The body straightens up and the left palm is on the right fist (Figure 5-116). Pivot on the left foot to change the direction to face the East while stepping forward to form a front stance, as the hand and fist strike low (Figure 5-117).

Figure 5-116

Figure 5-117

34: Turn Body, Second Kick with Heel

The right fist changes to a palm hand and turns over on top of the left palm as the palms face each other, while shifting the weight back onto the left leg, with right toe up (Figure 5-118). Step forward with the left foot into a front stance. The rest of the movements in this posture are the same as posture 28, but this finishes with a heel kick (Figures 5-119, 5-120, 5-121, and 5-122).

Figure 5-118

Figure 5-119

Figure 5-120

Figure 5-121

Figure 5-122

35: Strike the Tiger

The right kicking leg folds downward, to a toe step without weight, while the arms are lowered with the right palm facing the left elbow (Figure 5-123). Palms face down and travel together as you step with the right leg into a horse stance (Figure 5-124), and then continue to shift the weight to the right into a front stance. The palms are changing to fists and into a punching position with the right fist at the height of the forehead and the left fist under the right elbow (Figure 5-125). Loosen the fists and move the palms with the body into a left front stance, and then position the fists as before on the left side (Figures 5-126 and 5-127).

Figure 5-123

Figure 5-124

Figure 5-125

Figure 5-126

Figure 5-127

36: Step and Heel Kick

The hands cross each other in front of the chest and the weight shifts on the left foot into an empty stance (Figure 5-128). Lift the right knee into a heel kick and open the palms and separate them (Figure 5-129).

Figure 5-128

Figure 5-129

37: Double Wind to the Ears

The palms face up as you lower the hands downward while pulling back the kicking leg into a crane stance (Figure 5-130). Both palms make fists, and come up punching with both index knuckles facing each other, while the right foot steps forward into a front stance (Figures 5-131 and 5-131 front).

Figure 5-130   *Figure 5-131*   *Figure 5-131 front*

38: Crouch and Kick

The right ball of the foot pivots outward and the left foot shifts forward slightly, while the body lowers into a deep right cross stance, with the right foot flat on the floor. Coil the fists with the palm sides facing you, and cross them in front of the chest (Figure 5-132). Raise the body while separating the palms, and raise the left leg to a left heel kick (Figure 5-133).

Figure 5-132   *Figure 5-133*

39: Turn and Kick

Lower the left leg through the crane stance. Circle the left foot around the right foot and turn 360 degrees to form a cross stance facing Northeast (Figures 5-134 and 5-135). Then heel kick again to the East, with the right leg (Figure 5-136).

Figure 5-134   Figure 5-135   Figure 5-136

40: Advance, Deflect, Parry, and Punch

Lower the right leg, through the crane stance, with the right heel touching the ground, as the left hand is at the side of the left ear and the right hand lowers to the front of the dan tian (Figure 5-137). Shift the weight to the right foot, into a front stance, and push forward with the left palm while the right hand, palm down, rotates to the side of the right thigh (Figure 5-138). Bring the left palm over to cover the right fist in front of the right kua (Figure 5-139).

Figure 5-137   Figure 5-138   Figure 5-139

Step forward with the left foot into a front stance while rotating the hands forward and over to the left side, rolling them together to the side of the left thigh (Figure 5-140). Shift the weight to the right foot, raising the toe of the left foot while the left palm is thrusting forward and the right fist is pulling backward into a chamber at the waist (Figure 5-141). Shift the weight forward into a front stance and punch through with the right fist; rest the left palm on the right forearm (Figure 5-142).

| Figure 5-140 | Figure 5-141 | Figure 5-142 |

41: Apparent Closing

Identical to posture 9.

42: Embrace the Tiger, Return to Mountain

Identical to posture 10.

43: Brush Knee Twist Step

Identical to posture 11.

44: Grasp Sparrow's Tail

Identical to posture 2.

45: Oblique Single Whip

Identical to posture 3. You will finish facing the Southeast.

46: Part the Wild Horse's Mane

From the horse stance, shift to the left foot, and raise the right toe, in an empty stance, facing West. Bring both hands to the front, with the right palm facing up and toward you and the left palm resting on the right forearm (Figure 5-143). The left palm moves back toward the right shoulder and the right palm thrusts downward (Figure 5-144). Step to the right, through a 50-50 weighting on both feet in a horse stance into a right front stance, with the hands moving to face each other in front of the kua before traveling in different directions (Figure 5-145). Then shift the weight to the right foot and separate the hands. The right hand moves upward to the height of the right temple and the left hand moves downward to the height of the left kua. Attention is to the left (Figure 5-146).

Figure 5-143

Figure 5-144

Figure 5-145

Figure 5-146

Pull the left foot next to the right foot with right palm in front of the left shoulder, left palm thrust downward (Figure 5-147). Then repeat the movements on the left side (Figures 5-148 and 5-149), moving through a horse stance to a left front stance with arms open and attention looking at the low right hand. Repeat the movements again, shifting to the right side (Figures 5-150 and 5-151). Then, shifting to the left, bring both hands in front as shown in Figure 5-143 and repeat the movements again, finishing with a right front stance, as in Figure 5-151. You will finish facing the Southwest.

Figure 5-147

Figure 5-148

Figure 5-149

Figure 5-150

Figure 5-151

47: Fair Lady Works the Shuttle

This posture is another series of movements. Bring the left foot close to the right foot, and turn the body slightly to face West. The left hand moves below the right elbow, palms facing each other (Figure 5-152). The left foot steps forward into a front stance and the left hand travels to the left front, palm up (Figure 5-153). Shifting the weight to the right foot, with left toe up, rotate the left hand upward to the front of the head with the palm facing out, while the right hand follows the body's small circular movement to the waist with the palm facing up (Figure 5-154).

Figure 5-152   Figure 5-153   Figure 5-154

Still facing Southwest, shift the weight to the left foot and into a front stance, as the right hand pushes forward; the left hand remains above the forehead (Figure 5-155). Pivot on the left heel to face North, while both hands cross in front with palms open, the right hand thrusting downward and the left hand in front of the right shoulder (Figure 5-156). The right foot steps to the right and the right hand travels up to the right while the body turns 135 degrees to the Southeast (Figure 5-157). Repeat the movement that is shown in Figures 5-154 and 5-155, but with weight shifting backward to left leg and then forward to a right front stance, and facing Southeast (Figures 5-158 and 5-159).

Figure 5-155   Figure 5-156   Figure 5-157

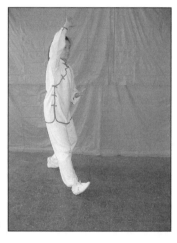

Figure 5-158   Figure 5-159

Repeat the movements shown in posture 46, Part the Wild Horse's Mane, Figures 5-143 through 5-146, but facing East. Repeat the movements in Figures 5-157 through 159, but facing Southeast (Figures 5-160 through 5-163). Continue, shifting to the other side, and facing Northeast and pivoting to face South, and turning 135 degrees to face Northwest (Figures 5-164 through 5-170).

Figure 5-160

Figure 5-161

Figure 5-162

Figure 5-163

Figure 5-164

Figure 5-165

Figure 5-166

Figure 5-167

Figure 5-168

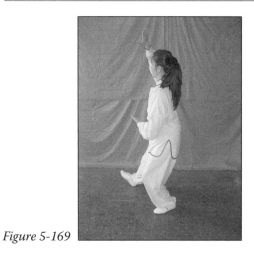

Figure 5-169

Figure 5-170

48: Advance, Grasp Sparrow's Tail

Keeping the hands in front of the body, step forward with the left foot, and then the right foot, with the heel touching the floor in an empty stance (Figure 5-171). Shift the weight to the right foot as the left hand pushes forward on the right wrist (Figure 5-172). Extend both hands and turn the right palm facing down and the left palm facing up (Figure 5-173). The rest of the parts of these movements are the same as in posture 24.

Figure 5-171 Figure 5-172 Figure 5-173

49: Single Whip

Identical to posture 25.

50: Cloud Hands

Identical to posture 26.

51: Snake Creeps Down

Shift the weight to the left foot with both palms extended to the left and facing down (Figure 5-174). Both hands move to the right with palms facing out toward the Southwest as the weight shifts to the right foot (Figure 5-175). Rotate the hands downward while the body is sinking down into a crouching stance as the palms face downward and sweep toward the left (Figures 5-176 and 5-177).

Figure 5-174

Figure 5-175

Figure 5-176

Figure 5-177

52: Golden Cock Stands on One Leg

Shift the weight to the left foot and face East as the right palm sweeps upward under the left elbow (Figure 5-178). Bring the right leg toward the left and raise the right knee while the right palm thrusts upward and the left palm thrusts downward in front of the right foot (Figure 5-179). Lower the right foot and shift your weight onto it, as the left palm tucks under the lowered right elbow (Figure 5-180). Bring the left leg toward the right and raise the left knee as the left palm thrusts upward and the right palm thrusts downward in front of the left foot (Figure 5-181).

Figure 5-178

Figure 5-179

Figure 5-180

Figure 5-181

53: Step Backward, Repulse the Monkey

With the left knee still raised, the left palm lowers to shoulder height (Figure 5-182). The right palm turns over face down and circles to the right side of the thigh, while the left palm pushes forward and the left foot steps backward (Figure 5-183). The rest of the movements are the same as in posture 15.

Figure 5-182

Figure 5-183

54: Fly Obliquely

Identical to posture 16.

55: Lift Hands Upward

Identical to posture 4.

56: White Crane Displays Its Wings

Identical to posture 5.

57: Brush Knee Twist Step

Identical to posture 6.

58: Needle at the Sea Bottom

Identical to posture 20.

59: Fan through the Back

Identical to posture 21.

60: Turn Body and Fist Strike

Identical to posture 22.

61: Advance, Deflect, Parry, and Punch

Identical to posture 23, with stepping forward on the left foot.

62: Step Forward and Grasp Sparrow's Tail

Identical to posture 24.

63: Single Whip

Identical to posture 25.

64: Cloud Hands

Identical to posture26.

65: High Pat the Horse

After the Single Whip, shift the weight to the right foot while turning the body to face the East in an empty stance, bringing the right hand up to the side of the ear as the left hand thrusts forward, palm up (Figure 5-184). The left palm pulls back into the left chamber while the right palm pushes forward (Figure 5-185).

Figure 5-184

Figure 5-185

66: Palm Strike to the Face

Shift the weight to the left front stance and rotate the left hand upward, palm pushing forward, as the right palm tucks under the left elbow and faces upward (Figure 5-186).

Figure 5-186

67: Cross Hands, Sweep Lotus

Pivot on the left heel inward to turn 135 degrees to face Southwest; with the weight still on the left foot, cross the arms in front of you, left arm on top (Figure 5-187). Keeping the right palm tucked under the left upper arm, lift the right foot to a crescent kick, sweeping inward and forward, from left to right. The left palm pats the right foot when the foot is at its highest point in front (Figure 5-188).

Figure 5-187   *Figure 5-188*

68: Brush Knee, Punch Toward Groin

Return the right leg through a bent-knee crane stance, and drop it to the ground with no weight, as the left hand moves to the side of the left ear and the right hand drops in front of the dan tian; weight remains on the left foot (Figure 5-189). The right foot steps forward and the left hand pushes forward, while the right hand circles in front of the right knee and to the side of the right thigh (Figure 5-190). Pick up the left foot and move it to just in front of the right foot, with no weight on the toe, as the right hand rises to the side of the right ear and the left hand drops in front of the dan tian area (Figure 5-191). The left foot steps forward into a front stance, as the right fist punches low; the left hand rests on the right forearm (Figure 5-192).

Figure 5-189

Figure 5-190

Figure 5-191

Figure 5-192

69: Step Forward, Grasp Sparrow's Tail

Identical to posture 24.

70: Single Whip

Identical to posture 25.

71: Snake Creeps Down

Identical to posture 51.

72: Step Forward to Seven Stars

Shift the weight to the left foot as the hands come upward with the palms facing each other, right below left (Figure 5-193). The right foot steps forward to an empty stance with the heel touching the floor, and the hands cross in front of the chest, palms facing away from each other. You are facing East (Figure 5-194).

Figure 5-193   *Figure 5-194*

73: Retreat, Astride the Tiger

The right foot steps backward to the right side and the hands push forward and downward, palms facing down (Figure 5-195). The hands travel while the body weight shifts to the right foot (Figure 5-196). The body continues to twist to the right, into a front stance facing Southwest; the right hand continues to travel to the right side of the thigh and the left hand is in front of the right knee (Figure 5-197). Pick up the left foot and move it toward the right foot, into an empty stance, while the right hand comes up to the right ear (Figure 5-198). Push forward with the right hand, while the left hand changes to a whip hand and pulls downward and backward to behind the left hip, the finger tips pointing upward (Figure 5-199). Finish with the body facing West, but looking South.

Figure 5-195

Figure 5-196

Figure 5-197

Figure 5-198

Figure 5-199

74: Turn Body and Palm Strike to Face

The left foot steps forward into a front stance facing West, while the left palm strikes forward and the right hand tucks under the left elbow, palm facing up (Figure 5-200).

Figure 5-200

75: Turn Body, Sweep Lotus

The left heel pivots inward, and right foot moves in front of the left, in an empty stance; the body is turning 180 degrees to face East. Both palms coil to the right side with the right palm pushing outward toward the South and the left palm near the right waist; the upper torso and attention are toward the South (Figure 5-201). The right foot rises to an outside crescent kick, sweeping across from left to right, while the hands travel from right to left; the hands and the foot meet in front of the chest, with the hands patting the foot in the air, left hand first and then right hand, both making as loud a sound as possible (Figure 5-202). The hands continue to travel to the left side and the kicking leg folds downward, finishing with the right knee up and facing Southeast (Figure 5-203).

Figure 5-201   *Figure 5-202*   *Figure 5-203*

6: Draw the Bow and Shoot the Tiger

The right foot steps to the right into a front stance, facing Southwest, while both hands travel to the right twisting torso. Change from palms to fists; as both fists come upward, the right fist is above the right shoulder and the left fist is at the right side of the chest (Figure 5-204). Punch both fists to the front with the back of the fists facing the left side (Figure 5-205). Change the fists into palms and roll the palms to face down, while shifting the weight to the left. Then, forming fists again, repeat the punching on the reverse side, in a left front stance, facing East (Figure 5-206).

Figure 5-204

Figure 5-205

Figure 5-206

Figure 5-207

Figure 5-208

Figure 5-209

77: Step Forward and Fist Strike

Rotate the left fist so the palm faces up and knuckles are to left; rotate the right fist so it is next to the left elbow with the palm facing down, knuckles forward (Figure 5-207). The right foot steps forward and the right fist punches straight forward over the left forearm (Figure 5-208). The right fist continues punching forward while shifting weight to the right foot (Figure 5-209).

78: Step Forward and Grasp Sparrow's Tail

Identical to posture 24.

79: Single Whip

Identical to posture 25. After these two postures, you are facing North (Figures 5-210 through 5-216).

Figure 5-210   *Figure 5-211*   *Figure 5-212*

Figure 5-213

Figure 5-214

Figure 5-215

Figure 5-216

80: Step Forward and Palm Strike

The left foot pivots on the heel to face West; while shifting the weight to the left foot, turn the left palm to face up and bring the right arm in and turn the right palm to face down in front of the chest (Figure 5-217). The right foot steps forward into a front stance facing West, as the right palm thrusts over the left palm (Figure 5-218).

81: Grasp Sparrow's Tail

Identical to posture 2. (See Figures 5-219 through 5-222.)

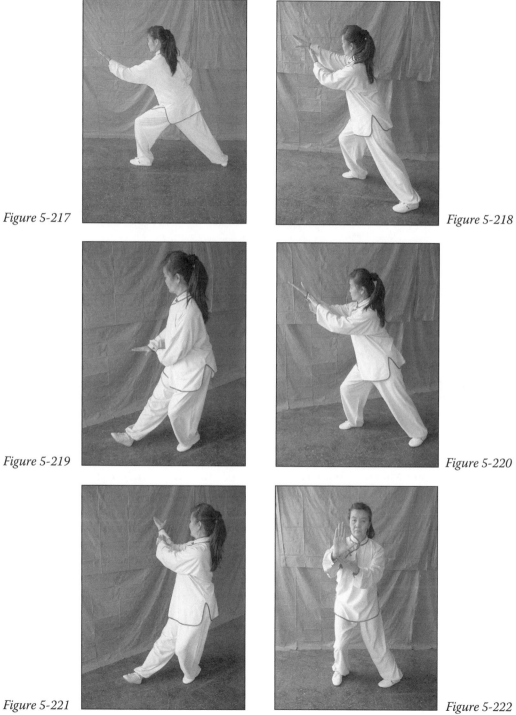

Figure 5-217

Figure 5-218

Figure 5-219

Figure 5-220

Figure 5-221

Figure 5-222

82: Single Whip

Identical to posture 3. (See Figures 5-223 and 5-224.)

Figure 5-223   Figure 5-224

83: Closing

Shift the weight to the right foot and turn both palms to face down, with attention toward the right hand (Figure 5-225). Bring the left foot closer to the right foot, to a shoulder-width distance, while bending both elbows and bringing the palms in front of the chest with the finger tips facing each other (Figure 5-226). Rotate both palms outward slightly and elbows inward until the finger tips point forward and arms are shoulder-width apart. Push the palms downward, to the dan tian area (Figure 5-227). Place both hands at the sides, palms facing back and rise gently to a standing posture, feet shoulder-width apart (Figure 5-228). The left foot steps next to the right foot and hands relax to the sides, as you return to the original Opening position (Figure 5-229).

Figure 5-225 *Figure 5-226* *Figure 5-227*

Figure 5-228 *Figure 5-229*

Push Hands

The trademark two-person interactive practice of tai ji quan is the Pushing Hands exercise, which is often simply referred to as Push Hands. It teaches tai ji quan practitioners to hold their own root while adhering to an oncoming force, neutralizing this force by redirecting it, and then returning this force to its source. With Push Hands, students can safely practice the four primary techniques and energy directions of tai ji quan: peng, Ward Off Upward; lu, Roll Back Inward; ji, Press Forward; and an, Push Downward.

A practice of Push Hands begins simply with two tai ji quan practitioners facing each other in yin-yang balance, with one in back stance and the other in forward stance. Both practitioners have their leading arms raised with the person in the forward stance presenting the forearm horizontally across the mid-section, while the person in the back stance places the leading hand lightly on the partner's forearm, palm toward the arm. The person in the back stance shifts weight forward into a front stance, and the front-stance person sits back into a back stance while keeping the forearm in contact with the partner's pushing hand, trying to feel every nuance of the push to be able to read any changes in direction or force at the instant they happen. This sensitivity of the Roll Back action, and reading the opponent's intentions with this sensitivity, is the most important aspect of the exercise. When the person rolling back has settled into a solid back stance, and before becoming unbalanced to the rear, he or she turns the upper body from the hips and redirects the oncoming force first past the chest and then in a circle back to the partner-opponent. At this point the process repeats in the other direction with the practitioners reversing the roles of Push and Roll Back.

Variations of the single-hand practice include learning to neutralize a push upward toward the face or one downward toward the groin area. Both forward and rear hand pushes are practiced with right and left legs in the lead position. When students become comfortable with the single-hand practices they move on to Push Hands exercises involving the use of both hands. In the simplest version the practitioners begin in the same postures as in the single-hand exercises, except the pushing person places both hands on the partner-opponent's forearm. As the person rolling back settles into the back stance, he or she lets the free hand slide out under the opponent's elbow. Reaching the point where the hips must turn to neutralize the push, the person rolling back simply pushes the opponent's elbow slightly to change the angle and then slides both hands on to the presented forearm and begins his or her own push.

The partners can then work on variations of the neutralization technique in which their free hand goes under both of the pusher's arms, over both arms, and between the arms. Decisions on which neutralization technique to use are made on the information received through the sensitivity used in the forearm being pushed.

It is important in the beginning of a study of Push Hands that the partners work cooperatively and allow each other to develop the techniques of sensitivity and neutralization. If too much focus is put on the pushing aspect of the exercise at the beginning stages of development, the sensitivity and neutralization techniques never have the opportunity to grow and mature. As these techniques are the necessary foundations of the softness that is the trademark and most unique aspect of tai ji quan, the entire object of Push Hands practice is lost when the focus is on the Push in the early stages of Push Hands learning.

When tai ji quan practitioners have developed the basic skills of Push Hands, they then begin to really push one another in their practice. This allows the rolling-back partner to advance the sensitivity and neutralization skills to the point of being able to apply them to an actual aggressive action being taken in his or her direction. The increase in pushing force must be gradual, allowing for growth of the defensive aspects of the practice.

After students are familiar with the feel of actual pushing in all of the preliminary Push Hands exercises, they are ready to enter into the free pushing phase of the practice. Now the pushing partner begins to add the directional press to the offensive arsenal—pushing and pressing upward and downward as well as forward, constantly changing angles. The rolling-back partner must then innovate the neutralizations to meet and deflect the variety of attacks and angles, while working to constantly hold the root in the face of a potential uprooting force.

It is extremely important at this stage of Push Hands development that both participants remember not to both push at once and simply try to overpower each other. This completely negates the object of the practice—learning to stick to an oncoming force, neutralize its impact, and return it to its origins. Although pushing and pressing are viable martial techniques in tai ji quan, they are used exclusively in Push Hands to avoid the use of solid strikes and throws, so that the sensitivity and neutralization skills of tai ji quan can be developed safely, without injury to the participants. Practitioners use Push Hands to begin to see all of the angles of their opponent's and their own stances and to move and hide their weak angles while attacking the weak angles of their opponent. Force is to be applied only after the opponent's force has been neutralized and shifted to a position where the opponent is nearly off-balance and has exposed a weak angle. Simply overpowering an opponent's strength is a technique of sparring or actual fighting and defeats the purpose of the Push Hands practice.

The very important developmental tai ji quan practice of Push Hands has become a sport that is itself growing in popularity. This sport allows tai ji quan practitioners to compete with each other while avoiding the potential injuries of actual sparring. Although a fine sport in its own right, due to the focus on winning, competitive Push Hands often defeats the purpose of the original exercise and becomes simply a milder style of boundary wrestling, sort of a gentle version of Japanese Sumo. Often even the champions of this sport rarely practice tai ji quan forms and practices other than Push Hands, but simply do their style of pushing as a type of wrestling, sometimes on the Judo mat. Consequently, this sport is often unrecognizable as tai ji quan and does little to build the reputation of the art. Practitioners of competitive Push Hands who don't also actually spar are akin to boxers who never box, but rather become expert in some kind of punching-bag competition. This is not to say that competitive Push Hands cannot be practiced with an understanding and application of the principles of tai ji quan, nor that sport organizations are ignoring the principles of tai ji quan, only that the art of tai ji quan should not be judged by the Push Hands wrestlers.

The Push Hands exercise is an important tool in the training of tai ji quan and a practical and safe method for practitioners to develop their skills of rooting, sticking, neutralizing, and uprooting. It a necessary phase in the development of all serious tai ji quan practitioners, while also being one of the most fun aspects of the art to practice.

Techniques of Push Hands

Single-hand exercise:

1   2

3

4

Both-hands exercise:

1

2

3

4

Free Push Hands techniques:

1

2

3

4

5

6

Uprooting the opponent in the Push Hands exercise:

Principles, Techniques, and Skills in Northern Wu Style Tai Ji Quan Fighting

Despite the thousands of fighting styles from around the world, there is a decided limit to the number of techniques that one human being can apply to punch, kick, throw, lock, or choke an opponent and to the number of defenses from these techniques. Fighting arts are differentiated by their training methods, principles followed, philosophy and purpose, and technique and style preferences. The unique quality of tai ji quan fighting is derived from its internal power development, strict adherence to the principle of softness, and the base philosophy of Taoism.

In the West, Internal and Soft are often thought to be synonymous terms to describe approaches, as are External and Hard. These terms—Internal, External, Hard, and Soft—describe different and separate aspects of martial action and training. Internal and External are the two different methods of power development. External development is basic athletic training with muscular contraction exercises for strength, aerobic training for stamina, and repetitive hand-eye coordination drills to develop unconscious reflexive action for speed. Internal training, in contrast, develops mind intent, weight momentum, a pumping of the body fluids, and energy discharge for strength, combined with relaxation and diaphragmatic breathing for stamina; wherever possible, speed is replaced by timing and positioning. What speed there is comes as a product of the relaxation. Every action is conscious—there are no unconscious reflexive actions. Hard and Soft are the terms used to describe how a fighter may deal with power that is coming at him or her. A Hard ideology dictates that one meet oncoming force head on and overcome it, force against force. The Soft fighter gives before the oncoming force and comes back where there is no force.

The confusion in these terms probably arose because the arts of Japanese Aikido and tai ji quan arrived in the West at least two decades before any of the other Internal martial arts, and both of these are Internal and Soft arts. In actuality, these martial qualities can be mixed in any combination. Each time a Southern Shaolin boxer, for example, latches onto the oncoming punch of an opponent with a tension-filled tiger claw, pulling the opponent's arm in the direction that it was already going, the boxer is performing an External Soft technique. On the other hand, the entire art of Hsing I Chuan is Internally powered, but only uses a Hard ideology. Tai ji quan derives its unique and subtle qualities from its combination of Internal and Soft, and Wu Style has long had the reputation as the softest of the characteristically Soft tai ji quan styles.

The softness of tai ji quan is characteristically seen in its ability to stick to an oncoming attack and, while rolling back, absorb and redirect the opponent's force, maintaining a solid root and hiding all of the weak angles of one's own stance. When the attack has been neutralized and the opponent led off balance and over-extended, the tai ji quan boxer then finds a weak angle in the opponent's stance and attacks there where there is no force. This is accomplished as conscious action, not unconscious reaction, and by finding and entering gaps in the opponent's consciousness. The Taoist principle of balance is maintained throughout by always becoming insubstantial where the opponent is substantial and being substantial when the opponent becomes insubstantial. The art of tai ji quan is named for this Taoist principle of yin-yang balance.

A tai ji quan fighter must learn eight basic skills in order to properly and effectively perform under the pressure of a martial confrontation:

1. Hold proper body alignments to create structural strength in the physical body that will keep qi from being blocked or wasted and help to maximize both the offensive and defensive powers of the fighter's body.

2. Pump the body fluids to create internal pressures that generate power when they are released through a relaxed body. Shifting the weight pumps the blood and coiling the muscles and squeezing and releasing the

lymph nodes in the hip creases and armpits pump the lymphatic fluid. Compressing and expanding the joints of the skeleton pumps the synovial fluid, which can be used to absorb and redirect oncoming force and to discharge power. A bowing and springing of the spine pumps the cerebral-spinal fluid and unifies the strength of the internal organs with the coiling and springing power of the limbs.

3. Calm the central nervous system to prevent either paralyzing fear or careless overconfidence due to excitement during an intense situation such as a martial confrontation.

4. Shift focus from breathing air to the energy flows in the body to gain control of one's qi.

5. Unify all of the energies of the body for focused power and rooting.

6. Create an unbroken, nonfluctuating, smooth flow of Internal power, which makes all physical movements fluid, continuous, deceptive, and hard to predict.

7. Combine and separate the four basic directional aspects of Internal power—Ward Off Upward, Roll Back Inward, Press Forward, and Push Downward—and use these directional actions to master all angles of attack and defense.

8. Shield one's psyche internally so that the opponent can't read one's intentions while retaining a clear state of mind in which one can read the intentions of the opponent and then lead the opponent somewhere other than where the opponent intended to go.

Fight training in tai ji quan begins with awareness, angles, and power. Alignments are learned, strength is gained, and knowledge of angles is garnered through stance training. Standing in the proper tai ji quan stances programs alignments and energy flow patterns into the body and teaches the student to relax in posture. Having a training partner push on the eight basic angles (front, back, left side, right side, and two 45-degree angles in both the front and back), while the practitioner holds various stances, teaches how to recognize the weak and strong angles of each stance. Power discharge is practiced by pushing on the various angles of the tai ji quan stances while compressing and expanding the joints, bowing and springing the spine, and using mind intent to discharge energy. A constant awareness of the here and now must be maintained during training. Training partners should work out a way to let each other know when they detect their partner's awareness drifting or gapping.

Tai ji quan practitioners learn to combine the skills developed in the basic exercises of Push Hands. When the basic skills of rooting, sticking, neutralizing, and uprooting have been learned through practicing Push Hands, it is time for the tai ji quan practitioner to begin practicing the martial techniques and applications from the tai ji quan form. Each movement in the form has one or more martial functions. Some of these functions are obvious, but others would most likely never be figured out without an instructor showing them to the tai ji quan student. Some small form movements have a wide variety of potential martial applications. The prime example of this is the many variations of deflection and striking that can be done with the whip hand, sometimes also known as the crane's beak, of the Single Whip posture. There are also a number of martial uses for the open hand in the Single Whip posture and together the hands in that posture can be used to split an opponent's arms apart or to catch a kick while striking the kicker's face. Techniques from movements like Deflect, Parry, and Punch are relatively easy to see in the form, but other techniques like the arm lock in Cloud Hands would be very difficult to detect and learn without the help of a competent tai ji quan instructor. Sometimes learning the martial application is the best method to understand the nuances and meaning of a movement. The waist bend in the Northern Wu Style transition from White Crane Displays Its Wings to Brush Knee Twist Step (posture 5 to 6) seems a bit incongruous and out of alignment until one learns the application and discovers that the motion is simply a Soft method of fading under the force of an opponent pulling one's neck downward. This action then leads to being able to reach between the opponent's legs and set up an effortless throw. Every movement in the tai ji quan form has an equally effective martial significance that must be studied and learned.

When tai ji quan practitioners can walk through the martial applications of the form, they begin to gradually speed up the actions of the practice. After being able to perform most of the techniques at close to full speed, practitioners of tai ji quan boxing should move into controlled contact sparring. It is only at this stage that they can test their abilities to maintain their principles of Internal power and Soft force while under pressure. This is the training through which tai ji quan practitioners learn to apply the methods and benefits of their art to their daily lives and to neutralize stress wherever it arises.

Fighting Techniques of Northern Wu Style Tai Ji Quan

Single Whip

Whip Hand Strikes

Whip Hand Strikes

Snake Creeps Down

Golden Rooster Stands on One Leg

*Lotus Kick (the crescent kick, also called
Sweep Leg Like a Lotus)*

Toe Kick

Needle at the Sea Bottom

Fist under the Elbow

Fan through the Back

Fair Lady Works the Shuttle

Brush Knee Twist Step

Cross Hands

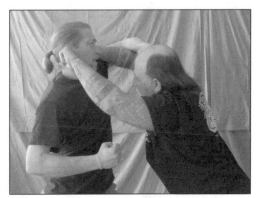

Double Wind to the Ears

Seven Stars

Heel Kick

Ride the Tiger

Punch to the Groin

Palm Strike to Face

Part the Wild Horse's Mane

Lotus Kick technique sequence:

1

2

3

4

Grasp the Sparrow's Tail technique sequence:

1

2

3

4

Play the Pipa technique sequence:

1

2

3

4

Apparent Closing technique sequence:

1

2

3

Deflect, Parry, and Punch technique sequence:

1

2

3

Cloud Hands technique sequence:

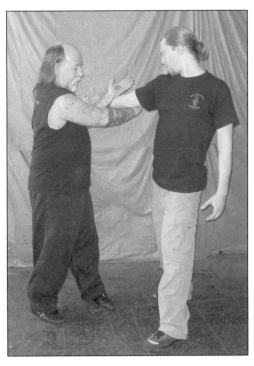

1

2

Two techniques—Closing technique, and the one called Embrace Tiger, Return to Mountain—can be used together as a sequence or independently.

Closing

Embrace Tiger, Return to Mountain

White Crane Displays Its Wings technique sequence:

1

2

3

4

5

6

7

Chapter 6

The Classical Sword Form

*Chinese calligraphy for "Sword"
by Tina Chunna Zhang*

THE HISTORY OF THE Chinese double-bladed sword may be traced back two thousand years as one of the earliest military weapons. There are eighteen well-known traditional Chinese weapons; some are rarely seen today. These traditional weapons are often categorized according to range. The staff and spear are long-range weapons best suited for the battlefield, while the broadsword and straight sword are short-range weapons designed for personal combat. During the Tang Dynasty (618–509 B.C.), the double-bladed sword became very popular, especially among royal officials and scholars. Many considered the sword to be the king of short-range weapons. It is relatively small and lightweight, but can be deadly in combat. A sword fight requires a high level of skill and a mental state that many civilized tai ji quan practitioners have not been trained to attain. Most people today use the sword as a tool of self-cultivation, mental and physical development, and for practicing a traditional martial art. Tai ji quan sword serves as a perfect practice through which one can learn to use the sword, which has its own beauty as well as deadly efficiency in combat.

The sword, like the other weapons used in tai ji quan practice, brings benefits to practitioners similar to those gained from practicing tai ji quan empty-hand sets. The sword form is a combination of techniques of tai ji quan and those of traditional Chinese sword training. Using a sword in a tai ji quan manner requires all of the

121

principles of tai ji quan to be used in every movement. The form has techniques that are very different from those used in Western-style fencing or by Japanese sword players, who use both straight and curved swords with straightforward techniques to chop, pierce, and thrust their opponents. Tai ji quan sword practice has to follow the rules of tai ji quan, using soft force and internal power and special sticking techniques with circular movement in practicing as well as knowledge of the different attacking parts of the sword in every movement. The best reasons to study tai ji quan sword form are to bring the mind and body into harmony and to learn to extend energy beyond the human body.

To correctly use the sword, practitioners must make it an extension of their body. They should simply extend their mind through the tip of the weapon and let their energy travel from the ground to their feet and be guided past their waist to the sword. There should be a smooth flow of energy and power from the feet to the tip of the sword. A whole-body connection moves the sword, not just the arm. The hand that holds the sword should be relaxed, not grabbing the handle in a deadly tight grip, thereby being able to use the flexibility of the wrist to control the sword and clearly show the different techniques of the weapon. The "sword finger" formed by the empty hand can be used to poke specific vulnerable points of an opponent's body and to balance the energy of the swordsman's own body to that of the sword.

Tai ji quan sword practitioners with a strong sense of subtle energy always experience the different "feel" of working with steel as opposed to wooden swords. Trees are energy-filled beings when alive, but lose their life force when converted to wooden forms. To work with a wooden sword, practitioners extend their own qi, or life force energy, through and around the wood of their weapon. Metal, on the other hand, is as alive in the shop as it was in the ground, and tends to absorb some life force energy from those who work with it. With refining, the metal gains energy, making highly refined steel the most energetic metal of all. Using a finely tempered steel weapon, the swordsman's qi mixes with that of the steel, creating a third and different type of energy. The swordsman feels the weapon's ability to cut and moves with it. The more refined the steel in the sword, the stronger the combined energy will be. Pacifist practitioners of tai ji quan often prefer wooden weapons in order to avoid the martial feeling of working with steel, but the would-be warriors among tai ji quan enthusiasts revel in this experience. Whether they enter into it simply to learn to extend energy beyond their physical limits or to develop ancient warrior skills, tai ji quan sword practitioners are able to also improve their empty-hand tai ji quan skills.

Northern Wu Style Tai Ji Quan Sword is perhaps the most graceful form in movement while having the most complicated techniques among all the styles of tai ji quan sword. One of the complexities of the style is the use of left hand and both hands in many techniques. Like the Northern Wu Style Tai Ji Quan empty-hand form, the sword form retains a strong flavor of the uniqueness of the system. It features a complex interweaving of movements and changes in directions, requiring that the foot work be very agile and alive.

The basic techniques of holding the sword and forming the sword finger of the non-sword-holding hand are shown in the photographs.

Holding extended sword with one hand

Holding raised sword with one hand

Holding extended sword with both hands

Holding raised sword with both hands

Here are the names and sequence of the postures of the Northern Wu Style sword form:

1. Opening 无极势

2. Grasp Sparrow's Tail 太极起势

3. Separate Sword, Seven Star 分剑七星

4. Step Forward and Protect the Knee 上步遮膝

5. Turn Around and Chop Sword 翻身劈剑

6. Advance and Cut Knee 进步取膝

7. Crouching Tiger at the Door 卧虎当门

8. Hang the Golden Bell 倒挂金铃

9. Needle at the Sea Bottom 海底针

10. Split through the Mountain and Take the Sword 劈山夺剑

11. Angle Pierce 逆邻刺

12. Turn Body and Point the Sword 回身点

13. Old Sage Cuts Off the Snake 沛公崭蛇

14. Turn Over the Golden Bell 翻身提斗

15. Monkey Stretches Its Arm 猿猴舒臂

16. Carry Fire Wood 樵夫问柴

17. Single Whip 单鞭索喉

18. Sweep the Sword 回身僚剑

19. Crouching Tiger at the Door 卧虎当门

20. Paddle the Boat 梢公摇橹

21. Push the Boat with the Current 顺水推舟

22. Mark the Point between the Eyebrows 眉中点赤

23. Step Backward and Cut the Wrist 反剪腕

24. Turn Body and Chop 翻身劈剑

25. Fair Lady Throws the Needle 玉女投针

26. Turn Body, Chain of Rings 翻身连环挂

27. Sword at the Door 迎门剑

28. Crouching Tiger at the Door 卧虎当门

29. Catch Fish at the Sea Bottom 海底擒鳌

30. Big Star Lifts the Pen 魁星提笔

31. Cut Backward 反手势

32. Step Forward and Strike Low 进步栽剑

33. Hold the Whip Left and Right 左右提鞭

34. Sweep the Falling Flower 落花待扫

35. Chopping Sword 左右翻身劈剑
36. Embrace the Moon 抱月势
37. Single Whip 单鞭
38. Sword under the Elbow 肘底提剑
39. Dredge the Moon from the Sea Bottom 海底捞月
40. Sweep a Thousand Soldiers 横扫千军
41. Alert Cat Catches the Mouse 灵猫扑鼠
42. Dragonfly Strikes the Water 蜻蜓点水
43. Bee Enters the Cave 黄蜂入洞
44. Carry a Musical Instrument 老叟携琴
45. Spirit of the Cloud Dance 云摩三舞
46. Fair Lady Spreads Flowers 神女散花
47. Pick Up Stars 妙手摘星
48. Strike in the Wind 迎风掸尘
49. Leap Over the Stream 跳涧截拦
50. Fish Leaps Over the Gate 左右卧鱼
51. Left Hand Sword Sweeps the Clouds 分手小云摩
52. Yellow Dragon Turns Over Its Body 黄龙转身
53. Search for the Snake in Grass 拨草寻蛇
54. Yellow Dragon Wags Its Tail 黄龙绞尾
55. White Snake Splits Its Tongue白蛇吐信
56. Clouds Cover the Mountains 云照巫山
57. Li Guang Shoots the Stone 李广射石
58. Embrace the Moon 抱月势
59. Single Whip 单鞭
60. Black Dragon Turns Its Tail 乌龙卷尾
61. Bird Flies into the Forest 鹞子穿林
62. Farmer's Hoe 农夫著锄
63. Chain of Rings 勾挂连环
64. Closing 合太极

Northern Wu Style Tai Ji Quan Sword

All the tai ji quan principles are applied in the tai ji quan sword form. Most of the time, the eyes follow the direction taken by the tip of the sword, but occasionally you will look at and follow the sword finger. To make the sword finger, the index and middle fingers stay together and the thumb rests on the bent fourth and little fingers. Whenever the non-sword-holding hand is free, it should form the sword finger.

This sword form faces in eight directions when performed; they are indicated in the descriptions of the postures.

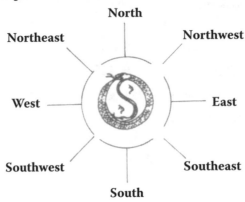

1: Opening

Start with a natural posture, facing South. The left hand holds the sword with the index finger (and middle finger if needed to stabilize the sword) in front and other fingers around the sword handle. Hold the sword behind the left arm, with sword tip pointing straight up. Looking straight forward and keeping the spine straight, sink the qi into the dan tian area (Figure 6-1).

Figure 6-1

The movements in this posture are the same as the beginning of the Wu Style Tai Ji Quan form. The sword form is traditionally learned after practitioners have managed the empty-hand form; the primary difference for postures 1 and 2 is that, instead of bare hands, you are holding the sword in your left hand, and the right hand performs as a sword finger.

Pick up your left foot, stepping to the left about shoulder width; weight is gradually transferred from the right to the center with the knees slightly bent and the whole feet touching the ground. Keep the spine straight, shoulders relaxed, and the crown of the head tilted upward (Figure 6-2).

Figure 6-2

Lift both arms to the front, left hand holding the sword loosely but maintaining a constant position so the sword moves with the rising arm. Hands remain shoulder width apart, and rise to shoulder height; the sword comes to horizontal, along the lower side of the left arm. The center of gravity rises a bit with the rising arms. Lower the arms to the starting position, at the sides of the kua, sinking the center of gravity downward again.

2: Grasp Sparrow's Tail

Step forward with the left foot. Raise both hands together to the center front. The left hand holds the sword flexibly so that it can shift in the grip and point downward and slightly backward, at a 45-degree angle. The right-hand sword finger rests on the sword grip (Figure 6-3). Turn the left heel to the left (outward) and simultaneously turn the body and the right foot to the right. Without changing the sword grip or position, allow the sword to move along the sword-finger hand to rest on the inner wrist (Figure 6-4). Step the right foot forward, heel first, to form a front stance, and turn the sword finger over so the palm faces down (Figure 6-5).

Figure 6-3   Figure 6-4   Figure 6-5

Shift the weight onto the left leg and pull back both hands to the side of the right thigh, with the right heel on the ground. The sword extends across the body at waist height and the sword finger is palm down (Figure 6-6). Turn the sword finger palm up and send both hands forward again, while coming into a front stance on the right leg (Figure 6-7). Move the hands horizontally to the right side of the body, while the weight shifts to the left leg and the right foot points the toes up (Figure 6-8).

Figure 6-6   Figure 6-7   Figure 6-8

Turn the sword finger so that the palm pushes forward, with the pommel (the knob on the hilt) of the sword continuing to rest on the right wrist. At the same time, turn on the right heel so the body shifts 90 degrees to face South (Figure 6-9). Continue the shift on the right foot, to face Southeast, raising the sword finger to the right ear and dropping the sword to just above the left knee (Figure 6-10). Step forward onto the left leg, to a front stance, and push the sword finger to the front, palm facing forward. The sword-holding hand travels backward to rest next to the left thigh, with the sword tip pointing up (Figure 6-11). Pivot the right heel inward and pivot the ball of the left foot so the left heel extends outward. Open both arms and follow the sword finger with the eyes (Figure 6-12).

Figure 6-9

Figure 6-10

Figure 6-11

Figure 6-12

Shift the weight to the right, into an empty stance, with the left heel raised. Bend both elbows to bring the hands in front of the chest, with the right sword finger in front and below the sword-holding hand (Figure 6-13). Turn the right toe inward to shift the body slightly to the left, allowing the left empty foot to move to the left. Drop the sword to the left knee, and raise the right sword finger to the right ear (Figure 6-14).

Figure 6-13

Figure 6-14

The left foot steps forward to a front stance while the sword-holding hand comes around the left knee to the left thigh, and the right sword finger pushes forward (Figure 6-15). The sword finger pushes downward (Figure 6-16). Shift the weight onto the left leg and bring the right foot closer in an empty stance. Raise the sword-holding hand to in front of the face and point the sword finger toward the ground, floating above the right knee (Figure 6-17). Now step forward on the right foot into a front stance, with the sword-holding hand remaining in front and the sword finger coming around the right knee to the right thigh (Figure 6-18). Repeat these movements on the left side (see Figures 6-14 and 6-15).

Figure 6-15

Figure 6-16

Figure 6-17

Figure 6-18

Pivot the right heel inward and pivot the ball of the left foot so the left heel extends outward. Open both arms and follow the sword finger with the eyes (Figure 6-19). Bring the left foot close to the right foot in an empty stance. Bend both elbows to bring the hands in front of the chest, changing the sword finger to hold the sword as the left hand becomes a sword finger. You finish facing South (Figure 6-20).

Figure 6-19

Figure 6-20

3: Separate Sword, Seven Star

Both arms open, palms facing down, with the sword now held by the right hand. Then the left foot steps into a front stance, and the right hand lifts the sword with a circular motion toward the face while the left hand meets the end of sword, palm facing away from the face (Figures 6-21 and 6-22). The left foot pivots inward on the heel. Keeping the weight on the left, step the right foot behind the left leg to form a cross stance, and sink the center of gravity. Chop the sword downward to the left, and shift the sword finger to the right wrist (Figure 6-23). Turning the right hand so the palm faces out and then up, lift the sword above the head in front of you. At the same time, rise up on the left leg and bend the right knee behind the left with the bottom of the right foot turned upward. The left hand extends outward and the sword finger points to the left front; you are looking at the sword finger and beyond (Figure 6-24).

Figure 6-21

Figure 6-22

Figure 6-23

Figure 6-24

4: Step Forward and Protect the Knee

As you lower the center of gravity and bring the right foot back toward the left foot, the sword lowers to point left and the sword finger rests on the wrist of the right hand (Figure 6-25). Pivot on the heel of the left foot and turn to face Northwest, with the right foot flat on the ground. With the sword finger resting on the right wrist, swing across the body with the sword to block in front of the right knee (Figure 6-26).

Figure 6-25

Figure 6-26

5: Turn Around and Chop Sword

The right knee lifts while the sword lifts, and the sword finger is next to the lifted knee (Figure 6-27). Turn the body 180 degrees without lowering the right leg, to land in a right front stance facing the Southeast. Chop the sword to shoulder height, with the sword finger pointing up, palm facing out (Figure 6-28).

Figure 6-27

Figure 6-28

6: Advance and Cut Knee

The sword finger lowers to the right wrist and the sword hand lowers to waist level, as you lower the center of gravity (Figure 6-29). Pivot on both feet to turn 180 degrees to face Northwest. As the right foot steps forward, the sword sweeps to the front at knee height (Figure 6-30).

Figure 6-29

Figure 6-30

7: Crouching Tiger at the Door

The left foot pivots inward on the heel and you gradually shift weight to it to form a left empty stance. At the same time, the sword arcs up to face level; the palm faces inward and the sword points to the West. The sword finger is on the pommel of the sword (Figure 6-31).

Figure 6-31

8: Hang the Golden Bell

The sword chops downward while the right foot steps backward (Figure 6-32). The left foot steps close to the right foot while you shift weight to the left foot and lower the center of gravity. The sword blocks in front of the left thigh (Figure 6-33). The sword arcs up and points to the front with the right knee raising up, while the sword finger, palm facing up, moves in front of the right ankle. You are facing Northwest (Figure 6-34).

Figure 6-32   Figure 6-33   Figure 6-34

9: Needle at the Sea Bottom

The right foot touches the floor, keeping the weight on the left leg, as the sword cuts upward and the sword finger rests on the right wrist (Figure 6-35).

Figure 6-35

10: Split through the Mountain and Take the Sword

With the weight still on the left leg, bend the right elbow so the sword circles from pointing downward toward the front to upward toward the back; the eyes follow the sword tip (Figure 6-36). Shift the weight to the right foot with the toes turning outward into a cross stance, and cut across the body to the right and backward, while the sword finger rises to point up and out at a 45-degree angle (Figure 6-37). The left foot steps forward to form a front stance. Chop the sword to the front at shoulder height, while bringing the sword finger to point straight up (Figure 6-38).

Figure 6-36   *Figure 6-37*   *Figure 6-38*

11: Angle Pierce

The right foot steps forward into a front stance. Bring the sword and sword finger together at the front of the chest, and then pierce forward with the sword, while the sword finger opens backward, palm up (Figure 6-39). The sword tip points slightly up.

Figure 6-39

12: Turn Body and Point the Sword

The right wrist rotates and bends to make a small circle with the sword so the tip arcs to point slightly down. Pivot inward on the right foot, and turn the body to the left, and then step forward with the left foot into a front stance. The sword finger points up. Your attention is on the sword tip, pointing South (Figure 6-40).

Figure 6-40

13: Old Sage Cuts off the Snake

Shift the weight to the right leg as the body leans backward, while bringing both sword and sword finger inward. Then circle the sword outward in front of you, and point it to the right and up, while reaching the sword finger outward to the left (Figures 6-41 and 6-42). The right foot steps forward with no weight as you sweep the sword downward to the center front and bring the sword finger to rest on the right wrist (Figure 6-43).

Figure 6-41   *Figure 6-42*   *Figure 6-43*

14: Turn Over the Golden Bell

Shift weight to the right foot and into a cross stance, and thrust the sword backward and slightly down while the sword finger points to the left and slightly up (Figure 6-44). Bring the left foot around beside the right foot; circle the sword tip up and then over to the left, to block low, with the sword finger resting on the right wrist (Figure 6-45). Lift up the sword and the right knee, letting the momentum turn the body to face West (Figure 6-46). The sword finger, palm up, points downward, next to the right ankle.

Figure 6-44

Figure 6-45

Figure 6-46

15: Monkey Stretches Its Arm

Lowering the sword to chest height, step forward with the right foot. Meet the sword hand with the sword finger (Figure 6-47). Then the left foot steps forward to an extended front stance, while thrusting the sword upward in the same direction, extending the right arm as far as possible. These movements are done with the sword finger on the right wrist (Figure 6-48).

Figure 6-47

Figure 6-48

16: Carry Fire Wood

The right foot pivots inward on the heel, then the left heel pivots outward, turning the body to the right and over. As you lean backwards, retain the sword in the thrusting position, with the sword finger on the wrist (Figure 6-49). Coming to an upright body position, lift the right knee and drop the arms to the front of the chest, with both elbows bent 90 degrees. The sword is parallel to the ground at eye level (Figure 6-50). You are facing East.

Figure 6-49

Figure 6-50

17: Single Whip

The right foot steps down and across to the right (Southwest) and into a front stance, while opening the arms. The sword thrusts to the front with the wrist turning inward and the sword finger points to the back (Figure 6-51).

Figure 6-51

18: Sweep the Sword

The body turns to the opposite direction, shifting into a left front stance, facing East. Rotate the wrist of the sword-holding hand so that the fingers point down and rotate the arm of the sword finger to face up with palm facing East (Figure 6-52). Adjust the right foot heel outward slightly to shift into a front stance, while chopping the sword over the shoulder and downward to chest height. The sword finger rises to point up (Figure 6-53). The right foot steps forward to form a cross stance as the sword arcs and sweeps to the back. The sword finger drops to the sword-holding hand level, and follows the sword's sweep, to point the same direction as the sword (Figure 6-54). The left foot steps forward into a front stance, while chopping the sword as described above, with the sword finger sweeping across to point up (Figure 6-55).

Figure 6-52

Figure 6-53

Figure 6-54

Figure 6-55

Repeat the cross stance and sword arc to right, and then the left front stance and sword sweep to the front one more time. Lift the right knee up and position the sword pommel above the knee, with the sword tip pointing up 45 degrees; the sword finger drops to the right wrist (Figure 6-56). The right foot steps down and across to the right into a front stance facing West. The sword sweeps across the body to point up 45 degrees toward the West, with the sword finger remaining at the right wrist (Figure 6-57).

Figure 6-56

Figure 6-57

19: Crouching Tiger at the Door

Shift the weight to the left leg, as the right foot steps in close to an empty stance. The sword arcs downward and then circles up with the palm facing in and the sword tip pointing West; the sword finger is on the pommel. Your body is facing South, while attention is along the line of the sword (Figure 6-58).

Figure 6-58

20: Paddle the Boat

The right foot steps to the right with the toes outward to form a cross stance. While holding the sword with both hands on the handle, thrust toward the right and back (Figure 6-59). Then sweep the sword all the way to the front, pointing the tip up at 45 degrees (Figure 6-60).

Figure 6-59

Figure 6-60

21: Push the Boat with the Current

keeping the sword in front but slightly lowered to waist level, step forward with the left foot (Figure 6-61). The right foot steps forward, into a front stance, and the sword pierces forward, with tip slightly up; the sword finger pulls backward (Figure 6-62).

Figure 6-61

Figure 6-62

22: Mark the Point between the Eyebrows

Without changing the direction the sword is pointing, slice across the chest to the left with the weight shifting to the left leg (Figure 6-63). Then slice across to the right, shifting the weight to the right leg (Figure 6-64). The sword finger stays on the right wrist through both slicing motions, and the sword tip is maintained as still as possible, with the attention focused through the sword tip and beyond. Power is transferred to and through the tip of the sword, as if aimed at the opponent's forehead. The left foot steps forward to a front stance, facing Southwest. At the same time, point the sword slightly downward with a bent wrist and raise the sword finger with the palm facing up (Figure 6-65).

Figure 6-63

Figure 6-64

Figure 6-65

23: Step Backward and Cut the Wrist

Rotate the right wrist and bend the arm so the hand is in front of the face. The right fingers are toward the face so the sword cuts backward; the sword finger is on the pommel (Figure 6-66). With the left foot, step backward and behind the right leg into a cross stance, keeping the arm positions (Figure 6-67). Attention is along the sword.

Figure 6-66

Figure 6-67

24: Turn Body and Chop

Shift the weight backward to the left foot and immediately pivot it on the heel to face East, lifting the right knee. Rotate the right wrist and drop the sword slightly, so the pommel is above the knee, with the tip pointing slightly up; the sword finger remains in contact with the pommel (Figure 6- 68). The right foot steps down and forward into a front stance. Make a short chop with the sword to the front, with the sword finger pointing up (Figure 6-69).

Figure 6-68

Figure 6-69

25: Fair Lady Throws the Needle

Shift the weight backward to the left leg and lower the sword so that the pommel faces the dan tian and the tip points up at 45 degrees; the sword finger rests on the sword grip (Figure 6-70). Slice the sword upward and to the left side and then, while shifting to the right leg, to the right side (Figures 6-71 and 6-72). During the slices, the sword blade is parallel to the ground. Step forward with the left leg into a front stance, and thrust the sword low about knee height, with the tip pointing downward; raise the sword finger to point up (Figure 6-73).

Figure 6-70

Figure 6-71

Figure 6-72

Figure 6-73

26: Turn Body, Chain of Rings

Drop the sword finger to the right wrist and pivot on the left heel, so the toes turn inward and turn the body 135 degrees to face Southwest (Figure 6-74). Continue to turn to face West, shifting weight to the right leg, and bring the sword up above the right ear, to point toward the front and slightly down. Lift the left knee and retain the sword finger at its lower position, inside the left foot (Figure 6-75).

Figure 6-74

Figure 6-75

27: Sword at the Door

The left foot steps forward and toes outward into a cross stance, while thrusting the sword downward with the wrist facing out; the sword finger rests on the forearm (Figure 6-76). Keeping the wrist orientation the same, circle the sword downward and across the body to point slightly up and to the left, with the sword finger moving to be close to the right shoulder (Figure 6-77). The arms cross in front of the chest. Step forward to bring the right foot into a front stance and slash the sword across the body to the front, raising the sword finger to point up behind the left ear (Figure 6-78).

Figure 6-76

Figure 6-77

Figure 6-78

Figure 6-79

28: Crouching Tiger at the Door

This posture is identical to posture 7 (Figure 6-79).

29: Catching Fish at the Sea Bottom

The right foot turns the toes strongly outward and into a cross stance, turning the body to the right 180 degrees, to face North. Both arms open, and the sword sweeps to the right as the body turns, while the sword finger moves to point up and out (Figure 6-80). The left foot follows the turning of the body, moving across the back of the right foot and around to the front, to land next to and just in front of the right foot in an empty stance, facing East. Twist the waist to the left and block with the sword on the left side, while lowering the center of gravity; the sword finger drops to the forearm for the block (Figure 6-81).

Figure 6-80

Figure 6-81

30: Big Star Lifts the Pen

Shift the weight to the left foot, and lift the right knee. Raise the sword above the head, with the tip pointing to the front and slightly down to chest level. The sword finger is in front of the right foot, palm up (Figure 6-82).

Figure 6-82

31: Cut Backward

Without lowering the right leg, raise the right foot into a toe kick. At the same time, chop with the sword to the right side at shoulder height; the sword finger rises to above the head and points up (Figure 6-83).

Figure 6-83

32: Step Forward and Strike Low

Putting the right foot down, shift into a close cross stance facing South. The right elbow bends and the sword crosses the body to point left and up at 45 degrees (Figure 6-84). Then pivot both feet 180 degrees, turning the body to face North in a more open cross stance. As you turn, the sword cuts downward across the body and to the lower right, while the sword finger points up at 45 degrees in the opposite direction (Figure 6-85). The left foot steps forward to a front stance and the sword moves through a tip-pointing-up position to a low thrust forward at the knee level; the sword finger returns to the forearm (Figure 6-86). You finish facing Southwest.

Figure 6-84   *Figure 6-85*   *Figure 6-86*

33: Hold the Whip Left and Right

The right foot steps forward, with the toe pointing in, to form an empty stance, facing Southeast. The sword moves to a standing position in front of the body, with the sword finger remaining on the forearm. Taking a two-handed grip on the sword, point the sword tip up and block from the right to the left (Figure 6-87). Then, without changing the stance and grip, move the sword to the right side; the left hand changes again to the sword finger, on the forearm (Figure 6-88).

Figure 6-87   *Figure 6-88*

34: Sweep the Falling Flower

Move the sword finger to point up and back, while stepping the left foot to the left. Then step with the right foot forward to the East, into a front stance. Thrust the sword forward at shoulder height, with the palm facing up (Figure 6-89).

Figure 6-89

35: Chop Sword

Shift the weight to the left leg as the sword chops down, facing North (Figure 6-90). The right heel pivots inward, and the left foot steps forward toward the right into a front stance, facing East, while the sword sweeps to the front with the wrist out (Figure 6-91). Pivot both feet and shift weight to the right leg to make a right front stance; chop with the sword, facing West (Figure 6-92). Pivot both feet again to turn your body to the left 180 degrees, and step forward with the right leg into a front stance facing East; sweep the sword upward to point to the front at shoulder height (Figure 6-93). The sword-holding hand is palm up; the sword finger is open to the back, palm facing back.

Figure 6-90

Figure 6-91

Figure 6-92

Figure 6-93

36: Embrace the Moon

The sword chops down to the left and is held in front of the chest in a horse stance facing North. The sword finger is on the right wrist (Figure 6-94). Shift weight to the left leg and step the right foot forward, with no weight, while the sword circles from left to right and the body leans slightly backward. The sword finger and the sword-holding hand are making small circles in opposite directions, crossing in front of the face (Figures 6-95 and 6-96). Both hands end their circle in front of the dan tian, retaining the empty stance. The sword points downward in front of the knee and the sword finger is on the right wrist (Figures 6-97 and 6-97 other side).

Figure 6-95

Figure 6-94

Figure 6-96

Figure 6-97

Figure 6-97, from the other side

37: Single Whip

Pivot the left heel to make a near-180-degree turn, to face Southeast. The right foot steps forward into a front stance, while thrusting the sword forward; the sword finger points to the back and slightly up (Figure 6-98).

Figure 6-98

38: Sword under the Elbow

The right foot steps backward and behind the left to form a cross stance. Lower the center of gravity, while pushing the sword downward parallel to the floor. The sword finger continues to point back and up (Figure 6-99). Come to an upright position, shifting weight to the right leg. Lift the sword with the sword tip pointing slightly downward to chest level, while lifting the left knee; the sword finger is above the left ankle, facing up (Figure 6-100). Keeping the same stance, chop the sword toward the right side, to waist level, while pulling the sword finger into the left chamber (Figure 6-101).

Figure 6-99 *Figure 6-100* *Figure 6-101*

39: Dredge the Moon from the Sea Bottom

Lower the left leg and step outward in an empty stance. Pivot the right heel, so the body turns toward the South. The body sinks down into a crouching stance, with the sword parallel to the ground and the sword finger coming around the body to rest in front of the dan tian (Figure 6-102). Sweep the sword to the left while shifting the weight to the left and into a front stance, facing East; bring the sword to the front of the chest in a two-hand grip (Figure 6-103).

Figure 6-102   *Figure 6-103*

40: Sweep a Thousand Soldiers

Keeping the two-hand grip, sweep the sword tip across to the left as the weight shifts to the right leg (Figure 6-104). Then sweep the sword tip across to the right with the weight shifting to the left leg (Figure 6-105). Shift the weight to the right leg and sweep the sword tip across to the left as the left leg rises to an inward crescent kick, toe up (Figure 6-106). The left foot lands in front of the right foot, and the right foot steps forward with the weight shifting to it (Figure 6-107).

Figure 6-104   *Figure 6-105*

Figure 6-106

Figure 6-107

Shift the weight to the left foot as the sword tip sweeps across to the right (Figure 6-108). Lift the right leg in an inward crescent kick, toe up (Figure 6-109). The right foot lands in front of the left root and the left foot steps forward into a front stance (Figure 6-110).

Figure 6-108   *Figure 6-109*   *Figure 6-110*

41: Alert Cat Catches the Mouse

Push the sword downward and parallel to the ground while changing to a single-hand hold on the sword. Pivot the left heel inward and the right heel outward to turn the body toward the Southwest. Thrust the sword downward, almost to the ground, while pointing the sword finger in the opposite direction (Figure 6-111).

Figure 6-111

42: Dragonfly Strikes the Water

Stand on the right leg with the left knee up, facing South, while lifting the sword above the forehead with the sword tip pointing to the East and slightly down, and the sword finger on the right forearm (Figure 6-112). Turn 135 degrees with the right foot pivoting on the heel and keeping the left knee up, while the sword tip starts the turn pointing down and then circles upward. When you finish the turn, bring the left hand to cup the back of the right hand to hold the sword. You will be facing Northwest (Figure 6-113). Straighten the left leg into a heel kick beneath the sword; drop the sword tip to point slightly down by bending the wrists (Figure 6-114). Put the left foot down and lift the right foot to the back while leaning the body forward and flattening the back. Bend the wrists again to point the sword tip up (Figure 6-115). The right foot steps forward while lifting the left leg with a bent knee pointing to the side. The sword finger leaves the double-hand grip to point up, and the sword does a short chop (Figure 6-116). In the sword technique in this posture the power releases through the front part of the sword.

Figure 6-112   *Figure 6-113*   *Figure 6-114*

Figure 6-115

Figure 6-116

43: Bee Enters the Cave

Still standing on the right leg, straighten the body and bring the left leg forward so the knee is lifted high in front. Sweep the sword upward to above the forehead, and point the sword tip toward the left and down to shoulder level; the sword finger rests on the right wrist. You are facing West, and looking Southwest (Figure 6-117). The left foot steps back and behind the right foot, turning the body 135 degrees to face Southeast; the sword hold moves with the body turn to point down on the left side of the body (Figure 6-118).

Figure 6-117

Figure 6-118

44: Carry a Musical Instrument

The left leg moves around the right leg and the right foot pivots, to face Northwest; weight is 60-40 on the right foot. The sword points directly to the front at chest level; the sword finger rests on the pommel (Figure 6-119). The left foot steps to the left and both arms open (Figure 6-120). The right wrist makes a circle to sweep the sword in a chop to the front and the sword finger returns to the pommel, while stepping with the right leg to bring the feet together again. The sword-holding wrist bends slightly to allow the sword tip to drop a few degrees (Figure 6-121).

Figure 6-119   *Figure 6-120*   *Figure 6-121*

45: Spirit of the Cloud Dance

This posture is a movement series that is done three times facing in different directions. The first one starts with pivoting the left foot and stepping out with the right foot into a front stance, turning the body 180 degrees to face Southeast, while chopping the sword to shoulder level and pointing the sword finger up (Figure 6-122). Use the ball of the right foot to spin toward to the right, following the turn with the left foot, to face Southwest; sweep the sword downward to point Southwest and bring the sword finger to rest on the right wrist (Figure 6-123). Pivot both feet and shift the weight to the left leg, to face East; chop the sword while stepping into a front stance and raise the sword finger to point up (Figure 6-124). Pivot on the left heel and lift the right knee, to face South; sweep the sword to the right passing the lifted knee to point West. The sword finger points West also, resting against the forearm (Figure 6-125). Lower the right leg and step forward on the right foot;

the left foot follows it to an empty stance. Arc the sword upward to face level with the palm facing in; the sword finger moves with the sword, to rest on the pommel (Figure 6-126).

Figure 6-122

Figure 6-123

Figure 6-124

Figure 6-125

Figure 6-126

Repeat the movements above, on the reverse side, as the second group of movements in the series of three. Step forward with the left foot into a front stance, facing the East, while chopping the sword and pointing up with the sword finger (Figure 6-127). Use the ball of the left foot to spin into a change of angle, following the turn with the right foot, and sweeping the sword to point Northwest and down, with the sword finger resting on the right wrist (Figure 6-128). Shift the weight to the right foot and chop the sword to point Southeast, with the sword finger pointing up (Figure 6-129). Pivot on the right heel and lift the left knee to face North. Sweep the sword to the left, passing the lifted knee, to point West. The sword finger rests against the forearm (Figure 6-130). The left leg steps forward and the right leg follows it to an empty stance. Arc the sword upward to face level with the palm facing outward; the sword finger moves with the sword, resting on the wrist (Figure 6-131).

Figure 6-127

Figure 6-128

Figure 6-129

Figure 6-130

Figure 6-131

Then repeat the first group of movements to complete the third group in the series of three (refer back to Figures 6-122 through 6-126). You will finish facing South.

46: Fair Lady Spreads Flowers

While the right foot steps backward into a deep cross stance, change the sword grip to the left hand. Sweep the sword to the left side with the sword finger in a chamber (Figure 6-132). Your attention follows the sweep of the sword tip.

Figure 6-132

47: Pick Up Stars

Bring the right leg to its standing position and shift weight to it. Lift the left knee and bend the left elbow so the sword points to the left and up at 45 degrees (Figure 6-133). The left foot steps to the side into a front stance, while the wrist turns inward, making a small circle as the sword cuts to the throat. The sword finger moves with the sword, on the pommel (Figure 6-134).

Figure 6-133

Figure 6-134

48: Strike in the Wind

Bring the left foot next to the right foot, facing the South. Keep the weight on the right foot, and bring both hands holding the sword vertically in front of the waist (Figure 6-135). Pivot the left toes out to the left and shift onto the left leg, turning to face North in a cross stance. Maintain the two-hand hold on the sword in front of the body (Figures 6-136 and 6-137). The right foot steps outward into a front stance, while the sword pierces to the East (Figure 6-138).

Figure 6-135

Figure 6-136

Figure 6-137

Figure 6-138

Repeat the movement on the reverse side, facing North with weight on the left leg and stepping with the right leg into a cross stance to turn toward the East (Figures 6-139 through 6-142). In the left front stance, the sword will pierce to the East. All the turning movements in this posture must turn with the waist.

Figure 6-139   *Figure 6-140*   *Figure 6-141*

Figure 6-142

49: Leap Over the Stream

Pivot the left toes inward and lift the right knee, while changing to the right-hand hold on the sword. Sweep the sword downward, with the sword finger pointing the opposite direction along the same diagonal line (Figure 6-143). Turn both wrists to face up for blocking, pivoting on the standing foot, to face Southwest (Figure 6-144). Simultaneously, with a quick jump, put the right foot down and touch the left foot in front of the right foot in an empty stance, while both wrists turn inward and arc down together. Finish facing West with the sword pointing to the front and slightly downward, with the right wrist bent and the sword finger on the right wrist (Figure 6-145).

Figure 6-143

Figure 6-144

Figure 6-145

50: Fish Leaps Over the Gate

Shifting to the left leg, step forward and across with the right foot, lowering the center of gravity into a deep cross stance. The sword continues to point West, reaching a position parallel to the ground and on the right side of the body as a block; the sword finger remains at the right wrist (Figure 6-146). Rise in the cross stance, lifting the sword hilt but keeping the sword tip low, and point up and back with the sword finger in a diagonal line extending from the sword. Pivot on the feet to turn the body to the left, while the sword circles upward, led by the sword finger that rises above the left ear (Figures 6-147 and 6-148). Facing Northeast, settle onto the left leg with a small step and sink into a low cross stance. At the same time the sword circles downward into a block to the left side of the body; the sword finger is on the right wrist (Figure 6-149). This posture must be done in a flowing motion.

Figure 6-146

Figure 6-147

Figure 6-148

Figure 6-149

51: Left Hand Sword Sweeps the Clouds

Using the left foot as an axis, turn to the right, to face East, maintaining a low center of gravity. The sword finger remains on the forearm as the sword sweeps with the body toward the right. Then the right foot steps across the left and on around 180 degrees, out to a front stance, while the sword sweeps to point to the front and down; you are facing Northwest. The sword finger points back, palm down (Figures 6-150 and 6-151). Shift weight backward to the left leg as the right foot steps close into an empty stance; the sword points front with the holding-hand palm up and the sword finger resting on the pommel. You are facing West. Change the grip to the left hand (Figure 6-152). Step the right foot forward into an empty stance; sweep the sword to the left first and then to the right, making a full circle with the wrist rotating to move the sword. Bend backward as the sword moves across to the right and then to the left. The sword finger meets the sword-holding hand in the center, and then opens to the right as the sword moves to point left (Figures 6-153 and 6-154).

Figure 6-150

Figure 6-151

Figure 6-152

Figure 6-153

Figure 6-154

Shift weight forward to the right foot and thrust the sword to the front with both palms facing up (Figure 6-155). Drop the elbows back and close to the body, opening the sword to the left and the sword finger to the right, palms up, while shifting the weight backward to the left leg (Figure 6-156). Then shift weight forward again on the right leg, bringing the hands together, palms down, to point the sword tip to the right and push the sword forward (Figure 6-157). Finish facing West.

Figure 6-155　　　　　*Figure 6-156*　　　　　*Figure 6-157*

52: Yellow Dragon Turns Over Its Body

Pivot on the right heel and step with the left foot around to the left and into a front stance facing East. Sweep the sword across and downward as you turn; the sword finger remains pointing West, palm to the side (Figure 6-158). Using the ball of the left foot as an axis, make a second 180-degree turn, counter-clockwise, to face West, with the sword thrusting forward at eye level and sword finger pointing back to the East; sword hand is palm up and sword finger is palm down (Figure 6-159). Shift weight to the right foot and pivot on the heel to make a 90-degree turn, to face South. The right wrist rotates inward, moving across and upward with the sword hand, so the sword tip points up next to the left shoulder. Lift the left knee (Figure 6-160). Step the left foot forward and out to the left into a front stance, facing East, cutting the sword downward; the sword finger remains in contact with the forearm (Figure 6-161).

Figure 6-158

Figure 6-159

Figure 6-160

Figure 6-161

53: Searching for the Snake in Grass

Shift weight backward to the right leg and open both arms in front of the dan tian, with palms down (Figure 6-162). Circle both arms inward to meet in the center; nest the right palm around the left sword-holding hand to hold the sword together, and slightly lift the hilt of the sword. Then, stepping forward with the left foot, tilt the sword downward (Figure 6-163). Slightly pick up the right foot while drawing the sword upward a little bit (Figure 6-164). The right foot steps forward into a front stance while both hands thrust the sword downward, palms facing up (Figure 6-165).

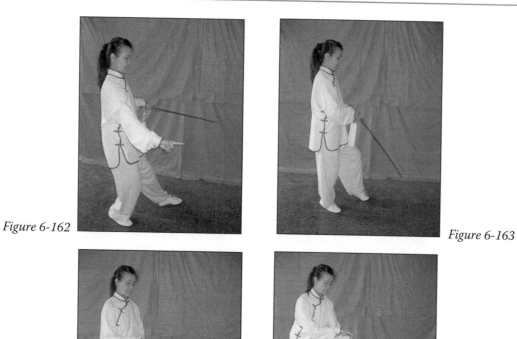

Figure 6-162

Figure 6-163

Figure 6-164

Figure 6-165

Repeat the same movements on the other side, shifting the weight backward onto the left leg to begin (Figures 6-166 through 6-168).

Figure 6-166

Figure 6-167

Figure 6-168

54: Yellow Dragon Wags Its Tail

Shift the weight backward into the right foot, raising the left toes. The right hand holds the sword. Sweep the sword across the body, from right to left, with the palm up. The sword points West, at the left side of the body and parallel to the ground; the sword finger rests on the right wrist (Figure 6-169). The left foot steps backward as the sword chops over the top and downward to the front, facing East; the sword finger points up (Figure 6-170).

Figure 6-170

Figure 6-169

Repeat the movements one more time on each side, starting by shifting the weight backward into the left foot with the right toes up. Sweep the sword, this time with the palm down, to the right side of the body, with the sword finger on the right forearm (Figure 6-171). The right foot steps backward while the sword chops to the front, and the sword finger points up (Figure 6-172).

Repeat this series of movements one more time to each side.

Figure 6-171

Figure 6-172

55: White Snake Splits Its Tongue

Shift the weight backward to the right foot and pull both hands toward the dan tian, cupping the right hand in the left to hold the sword with both hands (Figure 6-173). Step the right foot forward to the side of the left foot and bend both wrists to drop the sword tip downward to knee level (Figure 6-174). The right foot steps forward without weight, while lowering the sword pommel again in front of the dan tian (Figure 6-175). Shift weight onto the right leg, and step forward with the left foot to the side of the right foot; bend both wrists together to raise the sword pommel so that the sword points straight to the front at chest level (Figure 6-176). The left foot steps forward without weight, while lowering the sword pommel in front of the dan tian for the third time (Figure 6-177). Shift to the left foot, and step forward with the right foot to the side of the left foot and stand fully erect. The sword thrusts to the front at the forehead level (Figure 6-178). Pay attention, during this posture, to be sure that the sword tip points at three different heights in each repetition.

Figure 6-173

Figure 6-174

Figure 6-175

Figure 6-176

Figure 6-177

Figure 6-178

56: Clouds Cover the Mountains

Lowering the center of gravity, pivot on the left heel and turn the toes inward to prepare for turning 180 degrees. The right foot steps to the right into a front stance, while the sword sweeps across the body from left to right, to knee height, facing West, and the sword finger points to the back, along the same diagonal line (Figure 6-179). Using the ball of the right foot as an axis, turn 180 degrees, clockwise, to face East, while the wrist rotates to palm facing up, thrusting the sword upward and pointing the sword finger to the back (Figure 6-180). Shift weight to the left leg and lift the right knee, while rotating the wrist inward to make a little circle above the knee and bring the sword to the front, pointing up; the sword finger rests on the forearm (Figure 6-181). Finish facing East. This posture has to be done with smooth turning and direction changes.

Figure 6-179

Figure 6-180

Figure 6-181

57: Li Guang Shoots the Stone

The right foot steps backward and the body turns toward the right into a front stance, while both hands open up at the same time. The sword is lifted above the head with the palm forward; the tip of the sword points over the head and to the Southeast, and the sword finger, palm facing out, points in the same direction (Figure 6-182).

Figure 6-182

58: Embrace the Moon

This posture is identical to posture 36, but facing South (Figures 6-183 through 6-185).

Figure 6-183   *Figure 6-184*   *Figure 6-185*

59: Single Whip

Identical to posture 37, but facing Northwest (Figure 6-186).

Figure 6-186

60: Black Dragon Turns Its Tail

Rotating the wrist inward and moving the sword finger to rest on the wrist, circle the sword over and down to the front of the dan tian, with the sword tip pointing downward, while shifting the weight to the left foot and bringing the right foot close to the left foot in an empty stance (Figure 6-187). Step forward to a right front stance and continue from the last circular movement of the wrist to thrust the sword upward with the palm facing out; the sword finger remains on the wrist (Figure 6-188).

Figure 6-187

Figure 6-188

61: Bird Flies into the Forest

Shift weight to the left foot as the sword arcs up, palm facing inward at face level and sword finger on the inside wrist. The sword is parallel with the ground (Figure 6-189). While the right foot steps close to the left foot, thrust the sword to the West, holding the sword with both hands (Figure 6-190). The left foot steps backward and the center of gravity drops, as the hands move the sword downward to the dan tian (Figure 6-191). The weight shifts to the right leg, pivoting to the North, as the left foot steps around and close to the right foot. Raise the sword with both hands and thrust toward the West (Figure 6-192). The right foot steps to the right and back, while lowering the sword down as a block (Figure 6-193). The right foot steps forward and across the left toward the West into a front stance, while the sword is thrust forward; the sword finger points the opposite direction (Figure 6-194).

Figure 6-189

Figure 6-190

Figure 6-191

Figure 6-192

Figure 6-193

Figure 6-194

62: Farmer's Hoe

Using the ball of the right foot as an axis, spin 180 degrees and sweep the sword downward to knee height, pointed Northeast (Figure 6-195). Bringing all the weight to the right leg, stand upright and lift the left knee, while raising the sword above the head and thrusting toward the West; the sword finger is on the wrist (Figure 6-196). Lower the left foot to the ground, and pivot the toes outward, twisting the body around to the left into a cross stance facing South, while the sword circles downward and points across the body toward the left and back; the sword finger rests on the forearm (Figure 6-197). The right foot steps behind the left and out to the right into a front stance. The left hand moves to cover the back of the right hand to hold the sword in both hands, circling the sword up and forward, pointing West (Figure 6-198). Shifting into a horse stance, facing South, bring the sword to the front of the dan tian area, with both hands still holding the sword (Figure 6-199). Shifting into a right front stance again, separate the hands and thrust forward, with the sword finger pointing the opposite direction, palm up (Figure 6-200). Without changing the stance, rotate both wrists to face outward and raise the sword tip slightly (Figure 6-201). Express a strong Fa Li (energy release, hard yang power) with this forward position.

Figure 6-195

Figure 6-196

Figure 6-197

Figure 6-198

Figure 6-199

Figure 6-200

Figure 6-201

63: Chain of Rings

Shift weight to the left leg and lift the right knee, body facing South, while rotating the wrist and bending the elbow to circle the sword downward and back upward so that it ends by pointing West, with the wrist at face level; the sword finger meets the sword and rests on the pommel (Figure 6-202). The right foot lowers and then pivots the toes outward, turning the body 180 degrees into a cross stance facing North; at the same time, the sword thrusts downward to the right, and the sword finger points in the opposite direction (Figure 6-203). The left foot comes around the right foot to an empty stance, and the body turns with the pivot of the right toes to face Northeast, while the center of gravity lowers; the sword circles upward and over and downward to block to the left side of the body; the sword finger rests on the forearm (Figure 6-204).

Figure 6-202

Figure 6-203

Figure 6-204

64: Closing

Shift weight to the left leg and lift the right knee, turning slightly to face East, while changing the sword into the left hand and raising the sword so the pommel points straight up and the sword tip points straight down; the right sword finger is palm up above the right ankle of the flexed foot (Figure 6-205). Lower the right foot and, with a light jump, step forward with the left foot, toe up; at the same time, rotate the sword handle downward to the front of the dan tian, so the blade nests behind the elbow and points up; raise the sword finger upward, and follow it with the eyes (Figure 6-206). Shift weight forward on the left leg into a front stance, and move the sword to the side of the left thigh, tip pointing up; the sword finger pushes forward (Figure 6-207). Keeping weight on the left leg, pivot on the left heel and turn the right toes outward, settling into an empty stance facing South, while lifting the sword handle to point straight up next to the left ear and lowering the sword finger to the front of the dan tian (Figure 6-208). Shift weight to the right foot in a front stance; shift the sword slightly so the sword pommel points upward to the Southwest and move the sword finger to the right chamber (Figure 6-209). While the sword finger rotates over to palm up and rises above the head, push the sword pommel downward to the front of the knees; step forward with the left foot to be parallel with the right foot and shoulder width apart (Figure 6-210).

Figure 6-205   *Figure 6-206*   *Figure 6-207*

Figure 6-208

Figure 6-209

Figure 6-210

Continuing to hold the sword behind the left arm, move it to the side of the left leg, while lowering the sword finger to the side of the right leg; the legs do not move (Figure 6-211). The left foot steps next to the right foot and the center of gravity rises slightly, returning to the Opening posture (Figure 6-212).

Figure 6-211

Figure 6-212

CHAPTER 7

TAI JI QUAN TREATISE AND THE CLASSICAL TRIGRAMS

THE TAI JI QUAN TREATISE has been translated into English by several people. Some wording, and even some ideas, become a little different depending on the translator's literary ability, knowledge of Pinyin, and level of understanding of tai ji quan. Here, we present a translation that is as close to the original classical Chinese as possible, without adding or explaining the treatise in terms, polished or rough, of the English language. The meanings behind the original author's sentences are not always obvious or perfectly understandable. As long as you practice diligently and your experience of tai ji quan grows, you will definitely come to understand the tai ji quan classics better, and they will bring you a deeper understanding of the art.

太极拳论

王宗岳

太极者, 无极而生。阴阳之母也。动之则分, 静之则和。无过不及, 随屈就伸。人刚我柔谓之走。我顺人背谓之黏。动之则急应, 动缓则缓随。虽变化万端, 而理为一贯。由著熟而懂劲, 由懂劲而阶及神明。然非用力之久, 不能豁然贯通焉。虚灵顶劲。气沉丹田。不偏不倚。忽隐忽现。左重则左虚, 右重则右杳。仰之则弥高, 俯之则弥深。进之则愈长。退之则愈促。一羽不能加。蝇虫不能落。人不知我。我独知人。英雄所向无敌。盖皆由此而及也。斯技旁门甚多, 虽势有区别, 盖不外乎壮欺弱。慢让快耳。有力打无力, 手慢让手快, 是皆先天自然之能。非关学力而有为也。察四两拨千斤之句, 显非力胜。观耄耋能御众之形, 快何能为。立如平准。活似车轮。偏沉则随, 双重则滞。每见数年纯功, 不能运化者, 率自为人制, 双重之病未悟耳。欲避此病, 须知阴阳。黏即是走, 走即是黏。阳不离阴, 阴不离阳。阴阳相济, 方为懂劲。懂劲后, 愈练愈精。默识揣摩, 渐至从心所欲。本是舍己从人, 多误舍近求远。所谓差之毫锂, 谬之千里。学者不可不详辨焉。是为论。

长拳者, 如长江大海, 滔滔不绝也。朋履挤按采趔肘靠, 此八卦也。进步退步左顾右盼中定, 此五行也。朋履挤按, 即乾坤坎离。四正方也。采趔肘靠, 即巽震兑艮。四斜角也。进退顾盼定, 即金木水火土也。合之则为十三势也。

Translation by the Authors

Tai Ji Quan Treatise

BY WANG ZONG YUE

Tai Ji is born of Wu Ji, the mother of yin and yang. Tai Ji in motion is changing, it divides; and in stillness is harmony, it unites. Tai Ji neither goes too far nor falls short. When the opponent is hard, I am soft, this is called neutralization; when the opponent is soft and I go along with him, this is called sticking. To the opponent's fast movement, I react fast; to his slow, I follow with slow. These kinds of changes are innumerable, but the principle is always the same.

To practice tai ji quan one must learn to first manage the form in order to understand the principles and meanings of the art (zhao shu). Then know the energy and development of one's capabilities (dong jin). Then comes the highest levels of spiritual illumination, after which the free usage of tai ji quan technique will have been achieved (shen ming). One cannot suddenly understand tai ji quan thoroughly without having studied the art diligently for a long time.

In tai ji quan an intangible and lively energy lifts the crown of the head, qi sinks to the dan tian, and there is no leaning forward or backward. Energy and movement are suddenly hidden and reappear with equal suddenness. The body weight is heavy on the left, then becomes empty; as does the weight on the right, then it disappears. When (the opponent) goes upward, respond by going taller. When (the opponent) goes downward, react by going deeper. When (the opponent) advances, seem even farther away. When (the opponent) retreats, be even closer. A single feather cannot be added to it and a fly cannot land on it. My opponent does not know me, I alone know him. A real hero has no opponent and all tai ji quan comes from this thought.

There are many kinds of martial arts, and their techniques are different. Overall, they do not go beyond the concepts of the strong overcomes the weak and the slow yields to the quick. These attributes all come from abilities one is born with, and bear no relationship to one's effort of study and achievement.

Examine these words: "Four ounces deflect one thousand pounds." Obviously, this is not accomplished by strength. Observe how an old man can hold off a crowd of attackers and ask how he could do so with speed?

Stand like a balanced scale and move like a cart's wheel. If one sinks more weight to one side it is easy to move or follow at will; one who is double weighted is stagnant.

Whenever one sees those who have practiced tai ji quan for many years and still cannot employ neutralizing, and thus are overpowered by opponents, one realizes that these practitioners simply have not yet understood the fault of double weighting. If one wants to avoid this fault, one must understand the balance of yin and yang and that to stick is to yield and to yield is to stick. Yang does not separate from yin; yin does not separate from yang. Yin and yang complete each other. Only then will one understand *jin.* After understanding energy (jin), more practice will bring greater refinement. Silently absorb the knowledge and carefully ponder the strategy, and gradually you will gain the ability of what your heart desires to do. The foundation is giving up self and following others. Many mistakenly go for distance and forget what is near, or go for the abstract and forget the obvious, often sacrificing what is near for that which is in the distance. As the saying goes, miss aim by the width of a single hair and you may miss the target by a thousand miles. The practitioner must study the art in detail. This is the treatise.

Tai Ji long boxing is like a long river, or like an ocean, flowing smoothly and ceaselessly. Ward Off, Roll Back, Press, Push, Pull, Split, Elbow Strike, and Shoulder Strike—these are the Eight Trigrams in tai ji quan. Advance, Retreat, Look Left, Gaze Right, and Central Equilibrium—these are the Five Elements. Peng, Lu, Ji, and An are the Qian, Kun, Li, and Kan in the straight directions of the Trigrams. Cai, Lie, Zhou, and Kao are the Sun, Zhen, Dui, and Gen in the four corner directions of the Trigrams. Advance, Retreat, Look Left, Gaze Right, and Central Equilibrium are Metal, Wood, Water, Fire, and Earth. Putting all these together makes the tai ji quan Thirteen Postures.

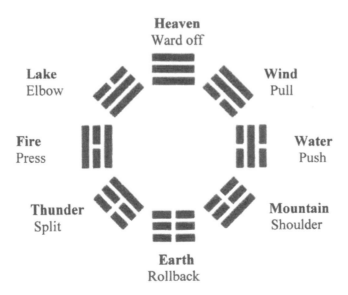

Tai Ji Quan and Pre-Heavenly Eight Trigrams

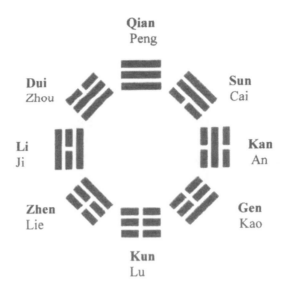

Tai Ji Quan and Pre-Heavenly Eight Trigrams in Chinese Pinyin

CHAPTER 8

THE PRACTICE OF NORTHERN WU STYLE TAI JI QUAN

Tᴀɪ ᴊɪ ǫᴜᴀɴ ᴘʀᴀᴄᴛɪᴛɪᴏɴᴇʀs sᴛᴜᴅʏ ᴀɴᴅ ᴘʀᴀᴄᴛɪᴄᴇ the art in their own dedicated ways, depending on their own understanding and achievement, and according to the Tai Ji Quan Treatise, which Chinese people have considered and still consider a guide to following and developing the skills of tai ji quan. There are three steps in this achievement:

1. *Zhao shu*—knowing tai ji quan techniques

2. *Dong jin*—understanding internal energy and gaining tai ji quan power

3. *Shen ming*—having a spirit that is calm, happy, relaxed, and free to use flowing techniques at will

Zhao Shu 著熟

Knowing tai ji quan techniques is the first step is learning the tai ji quan form. The process of developing this knowledge may take a long time for people who are not experienced in learning movement patterns, but normally it takes only a few months. It is not a matter of the time it takes. It is a matter of learning the structure of the form correctly. Posture by posture, movement by movement, all the details have to be learned well at the very beginning. At this stage of practice, all of the postures should become very clear and accurate. One of the Northern Wu Style traditions is practicing with precision in every movement. Where do this hand and foot go, and which direction do they move? We are learning a form that is neither a dance form of expression nor just an appearance art; it is a martial arts form, and all of the movements have martial application, along with serving the purpose of cultivating energy. The postures are like bricks and tools that must be managed and utilized individually. We put them together to build a strong and solid mansion that we can live in comfortably and safely. Therefore, the fundamental training, the basic internal aspects, should be learned from day one; these include breathing, lowering the center of gravity, relaxing, the trademark softness of the style, and the simple martial application of every posture.

Song, softness, is a word that tai ji quan practitioners hear from their teachers many times. It requires looseness in all the joints and muscles, along with mental relaxation. If one moves in a hard way, it is not a tai ji quan at all; on the other hand, if one moves in a too-soft manner without any strength, it is limpness, not softness. Experienced tai ji quan practitioners may move in a way that looks soft, but there is force in their movements. It is a soft and flexible strength. One should let the energy easily go through the whole body from the bottom upward.

In Chinese translation, *song* also has another meaning: "pine tree." It means that the tai ji quan practitioner should be like a pine tree that is standing straight, with a strong attitude. When the snow comes, the pine tree takes it with strong rooting, not shaking and moving, and very centered in its manner. All the branches of the pine tree hold the snow to the limits of their strength and then gently bend, allowing the snow to fall off as the trunk of the tree maintains its upright stance. With tai ji quan, practitioners will find and understand their center, which will give them their best structure for both releasing maximum power and maintaining their bones and spine in a natural, healthy condition.

Training oneself to understand yin and yang theory in tai ji quan practice is an important aspect of the art. Fullness and emptiness in both physical and energy movements must be learned in the early stages of practice. When one moves, all the joints in the body are connected, and the compression and expansion motions of the skeletal joints flow continuously from one to the other during the form practice. The weight shifting, from empty to full, and then from full to empty, are the basic tai ji quan techniques and a first step to understanding the harmonious changes of yin and yang. Practitioners should pay close attention to the changes in their form and practice slowly to see how the changes occur. Movement and energy always change gradually from substantial to insubstantial and from insubstantial to substantial.

Flexibility of the joints is an important training point in tai ji quan. The bigger the range of motion, the greater one's power can be gathered and released. The heath aspect of flexibility will help people deal with the aging process, cure joint diseases, and enable life-long agility. Training a little harder on low stances and crane stances helps to build and maintain flexibility. With flexible joints one feels much younger and stronger while also attaining the benefit of better energy flow.

Practicing the form, it is important to keep in mind one of the classic tai ji quan rules: "One part moves, all parts move; one part stops, all parts stop." The whole body moves at the same time; never are just the arms or feet moving. When the feet move, the legs, waist, spine, shoulders, arms, and hands all move too. The eyes follow where the hands go, not by staring at the hands but by following the direction of the hands and looking beyond to where the energy goes. More important, the eyes are the window of the soul. They reflect the spirit, move with one's energy, and build concentration during the practice. The *yi*, or mind intent of the practitioner, is brought to life through the eyes. The eyes also play a role in keeping balance and maintaining focus, and can be used for misleading the opponent in sparring or fighting. Basic tai ji quan movement requires that every part of the body is deeply coordinated and simultaneously moving together.

The greatest tai ji quan results come only from correct and focused practice with correct body mechanics. The best way to learn is by doing, and thinking about what you are doing while you are doing it. Practicing at least thirty minutes daily is recommended. Of course, the more time practitioners are willing and able to spend, the greater the benefits for their body and mind. But more important is how one practices tai ji quan—that the practice is efficient and cultivates energy and relaxes the body and soul while also developing self-defense technique. Like other kinds of exercise, one can start with a warm-up using some basic martial art training principles (described in Chapter 3). Then review and practice single postures one by one, which you have learned in the Northern Wu Style Tai Ji Quan form, but are not doing perfectly yet. Follow that with practice of the whole form, or as much of it as you know so far, slowly and accurately, while carefully feeling how each movement moves the entire body's energy. Trying to fully use the valuable time spent in practice and concentrating on what the body and energy are doing will give great results and a marked improvement in skills.

When practicing forms and/or martial applications, it is important to pay special attention to the six harmonies. There are three external and three internal harmonies. The three external harmonies are the harmony of shoulder and *kua* (pelvic area), harmony of elbow and knee, and harmony of hands and feet. These corresponding body parts must be kept in line with each other throughout all movements. The three internal harmonies are, the harmony of the mind and *yi* (intent or will power), harmony of the *yi* and *qi* (life force energy), and the harmony of *qi* and *li* (strength or power). The three internal harmonies are not easy to understand at the beginning of tai ji quan training and a long period of regular practice is needed to develop them. But a practice of the internal harmonies is an initial stage of internal power development.

Dong Jin 懂劲

Understanding internal energy and gaining tai ji quan power is the second step toward achieving tai ji quan expertise. Jin, in Chinese, means strength, especially internal strength with power. To understand and gain internal power is perhaps the key or main reason for practicing tai ji quan, but one should not expect to become proficient at this practice in a short time. It will definitely take longer than one would imagine, and some of us may take a whole lifetime to achieve this goal.

Northern Wu Style Tai Ji Quan was founded by an imperial guard who was one of the most famous martial arts fighters of his day. He was known for his extremely fine skill of neutralization, which is the differentiating point of tai ji quan concepts and strategy from other martial arts. Learning tai ji quan is learning how to neutralize.

Internal power is a soft and invisible power. It must come from inside one's body with each joint connected and skin, muscles, and skeletal joints loose. Internal breathing is also a necessary component. All tai ji quan power rises from the earth, to the feet connected to the earth; this power is then controlled by the waist and delivered through the spine into the shoulders, arms, and hands. The softness, looseness, and connection of all parts of a body that is well rooted into the ground is the foundation of internal power. Tai ji quan footwork moves one's energy as well as makes the connection to the ground, from where one's power is derived.

Proper training methods and maintaining the principles in Wu Style Tai Ji Quan form practice are essential for gathering energy, gaining and maintaining a maximum range of motion, rooting, and soft power development. It is impossible for one to fully understand the depths of the art of tai ji quan just by knowing the form. Practitioners must realize that knowing the form is just the beginning step in the long journey of tai ji quan life. After learning the entire form, one needs frequent practice of the form to understand the principles at a deep level. There are ways to practice the form that help to develop this understanding—for example, practicing the form with attention to every part of the body in every move in order to make full energy circle through the entire body. The more one practices the form, the softer one will become, and the more one will understand both the body's own energy and the form on a deeper level. This softness, not limpness, will start to dominate the movements and to make these movements more alive. When the whole body gradually, evenly, and softly moves as a whole, with all the joints and ligaments loose and open, but connected, soft power will be gathered inside of the body. This training in extreme softness can produce its opposite, extreme hardness, which is then like "steel concealed in the cotton." True internal power will then start to establish itself inside the body and the form will become more useful and powerful for them.

Tai ji quan is a moving art; it is like an ocean in which the water flows in waves, moving all the time. Stiffness, numbness, and hard muscle work do not belong in this practice, and absolutely should not be seen either in appearance or exist unseen deep inside the body.

To develop soft power, one must always stay grounded during practice. Northern Wu Style empty-hand and weapon forms are practiced with footwork that often keeps the feet parallel. Each step in the footwork patterns must be firmly grounded. This is relatively difficult training, compared to other tai ji quan styles, but it is an extremely effective method of rooting, which helps the feet connect to the ground with each step. When stepping forward, one first sinks the center of gravity by loosening the hip or *kua* area, being careful not to let the body and energy rise while doing this. When placing the foot on the ground, the heel touches first and then the weight rolls to the toes. At the end of this roll, the entire foot is connected to the ground. This way of stepping is connecting, stable, and balanced; it is light footwork, not heavy marching. This special footwork training for deep rooting works in conjunction with the practitioner's low diaphragmatic breathing and the lowering of the center of gravity to keep the body continually stable and grounded. When practitioners have developed this kind of connection and energy flow, the releasing of power becomes the next subject in their tai ji quan study. At this time in the regimen a weapon form could be added to the training in order to develop a higher level of control with stronger *yi*, or mind intent, and increased energy flow.

In order to help discover and understand how tai ji quan has both yin and yang power, Northern Wu Style uses the compression and expansion of the joints in its own unique way in every move. Looseness and softness are key to gathering maximum power from every part of the body. When people only know how to use hard power, they limit the amount of power they are capable of attaining, but if they know how to soften and loosen the spaces in all of their joints, tendons, and ligaments, while keeping them connected, they can gather the maximum amount of power in their body and then release this power in a short-range explosion by using all of these body parts simultaneously. This style of tai ji quan has a yin and yang power that looks peaceful and soft like water while being hard and strong like an ocean wave. The power of this art is hard inside and soft outside. When the practitioner is in motion, this power seems to appear and disappear quickly.

The yin and yang opposites of power must always receive attention during practice. Whenever one has the front power, he or she must also have the back power that is rooted. An example of this is seen in the posture "Brush Knee Twist Step." Also, when one's power goes upward, he or she must sink the body downward, as in the posture "Fan through the Back." Because yin-yang balanced power is a natural human power that allows energy to flow through the entire body, it allows the practitioner of tai ji quan to develop a maximum range of power and provides a method for releasing this power.

Using the center of the body—the waist, the dan tian, or energy storage point, and the kua, or pelvic region—is an important training step in learning to build energy and release power. One begins by sinking the qi, or energy, to the dan tian area, which is located one to three inches below the navel. Traditional Chinese martial artists believed in Taoist inner alchemy practices that taught that the dan tian is the energy center of the human body. It doesn't really matter whether you believe the dan tian theory, but practicing centralized power and making the connection between the upper body and lower body is a simple yet important aspect of tai ji quan practice. This is necessary for the coordination of movement, inner organ massage, and whole-body power. In Wu Style Tai Ji Quan practice, including forms, weapons, Push Hands, and sparring, it is essential that all body movement initiate from the dan tian area with the hands, feet, and other parts of the body moving simultaneously. This allows the entire body to work as one concentrated unit.

Specific training is required to connect the spine to the kua. This connection facilitates full-body movement. When one lowers the center of gravity and sinks downward by "sitting in the kua," the feet are deeply connected with the earth, and the dan tian area is storing energy, while simultaneously turning and rotating the spine through its connection to the kua. The spine then directs this movement to the rest of the body. The more opening one has in the kua area, the more energy one will have flowing through the area, thus creating the tai ji quan power—the secret inner power that can then be gathered and released strongly and quickly. In the movements of Northern Wu Style Tai Ji Quan this inner power is not obviously seen in the appearance of the postures, but dan tian and kua power are internally trained by every single movement and are happening all the time. Training to open the kua area will open the biggest joint of the body; this is also the biggest gate for energy flow and the focal point for many significant benefits of tai ji quan practice. Through the opening of the kua practitioners find that internally they are opening and loosening more than ever before, all of their internal organs are getting massaged, and their blood circulation is much improved by the flow of their own qi. Externally, their physical ability has increased; they are able to do wider stances that cover a larger range and their reach is higher and farther.

As the central skeletal structure that supports the upper body, our spine carries most of the weight of the head, chest, and arms. Together with the muscles and ligaments of the back, the spinal column enables us to walk upright. Besides that, the spine controls, moves, and protects a major portion of the central nervous system. Maintaining a straight, stable, and healthy spine is an important aspect of the anti-aging benefits of tai ji quan training. The overall health of an elderly person is often gauged by the integrity of his or her spinal alignment. The old duffer with the dead straight spine is looked upon as an example of mature virility, while his bent-over bookworm buddy is considered to be an ode to the deterioration of aging. Years of improper sacral alignment, where the spine meets the hips, leads to compressed vertebrae in the lower lumbar spine and chronic low back pain. The upper buttocks area must be kept tucked under and straight if mid-life pain and loss of motion are to be avoided. Overtucking must be avoided also, as this limits the dropping of the inguinal crease and reduces motion in the area. This finely tuned tucking of the hips must be attained thoroughly if one wants to avoid the stiff and lumbering gait exhibited by many senior citizens. Maintaining the lift from the head and top of the spine to keep the middle and upper spine straight is also imperative, as the classic scholar's curve to the upper thoracic and cervical spine applies pressure to one's heart and lungs, which could lead to a shortened life span. It is important for tai ji quan practitioners to remember that the relaxing of their shoulders, chest, and abdomen is never to be at the expense of the integrity of their straight spinal alignment. A finely tuned straight spinal alignment is a necessary aspect of both the health and martial applications of tai ji quan.

The Push Hands exercise brings the practitioner from individual training to practicing with partners. It is an opportunity to learn the skill of neutralization in combat, without the use of deadly force. This is also an important training procedure for learning to listen and feel other people's energy, and for using tai ji quan's yin-yang balance and power to externally structure the forms and increase internal power. Working with partners perfects one's neutralization and energy release skills, and it teaches the practitioner how to borrow the opponent's power and use it against him or her. Timing and neutralization become more important than just using muscle power. Rooting and balancing are practically trained in this special exercise. Push Hands in tai ji quan training helps one to understand the forms and energy in a specific way. This two-person drill helps practitioners feel each other's force, experience some aspects of combat, and learn to release short-range power. Also, the patterns of Push Hands have been designed to practically train the tai ji quan techniques of Ward Off, Roll Back, Press, and Push. One must be more concerned with one's own balance, control, and use of internal power than in just using muscle power to win a match. This is not easy to do; solid Push Hands technique takes a great deal of time and effort. Winning in a Push Hands competition is neither a goal of tai ji quan practice nor the proof of attaining high levels of the art. One cannot truly understand tai ji quan by focusing practice on Push Hands alone. Training in the forms, combat techniques, sparring, and on developing yi and qi are equally important. The magic power of tai ji quan comes from regular and intelligent practice.

The yi, or mind intent, is a specialty in tai ji quan and has to be established and developed throughout the practice. Yi training in tai ji quan practice is a very special process and very different from other martial arts training of the yi. It is not the concept of making your mind strong in order to overpower the weak. Internal yi training emphasizes training one's full confidence, developing a relaxed focus, gaining the endurance that comes with increased will power, and learning how to apply the principle of the soft overcoming the hard. An example of internal yi is seen in how a fighter applies developed yi to take down an opponent who is both physically bigger and stronger. An even more striking example may be the yi that enables a child born with a negative physical condition to handle him- or herself well in life and achieve life goals. Yi training in tai ji quan involves finding the balance in physical movement, staying focused during practice, and maintaining emotional control. Through this training one learns to relax and calmly deal with everything that happens in daily life, in a positive way, both good occurrences and bad. Just as one learns to control body movements, one must learn to handle life issues in a controlled manner. When one's mind is clear and calm, the body is relaxed and calm.

Traditional Chinese medicine is the root of tai ji quan practice and the theory upon which its development is based. One does not have to become a TCM doctor to learn tai ji quan, but knowing some important related acupuncture points and meridian lines in the body is a helpful tool in understanding the energy pathways of the body. If one knows where the twelve meridians pass through the body, where the qi energy flows through the body, and where the major meridian points (such as, from bottom to top, Yong Quan, Hui Yin, Qi Hai, Ming Men, Tian Zong, Lao Gong, He Gu, and Bai Hui) are located, it is much easier to stimulate these acupuncture points during the practice. It will also be easer to link these points together in your mind and be aware of what is happening during practice. In this way, you can move energy in the desired manner so that it reaches all of these acupuncture points, which are important gates for opening up the entire body.

The acupuncture meridian points of tai ji quan: Yong Quan—KI1, Hui Yin—RN1, Qi Hai—RN6, Ming Men—DU4, Tian Zong—SI11, Lao Gong— PC8, He Gu—LI4, Bai Hui—DU20

It is apparent that practicing tai ji quan to build and maintain one's health is a very good idea. Many tai ji quan practitioners have lived to a very advanced age. Simply practicing tai ji quan for health may very well be the best type of exercise for most people. There are no harsh movements or physical difficulty in the postures that normal adults could not handle. Practicing Northern Wu Style Tai Ji Quan, paying strict attention to the principles of this style, allows practitioners to work deep inside their body, massaging the deeper layers of their tissues and inner organs. Each practice session must be conducted carefully, with full and complete movements that are done correctly. For example, when opening, one must open all the way and when closing, one must close completely. In this way, maximum exercise benefit is received throughout each movement. Practicing slowly and with an unbroken flow of movement and energy are the keys to managing the form in the initial stages of learning; these are also the keys to promoting one's overall skills and health. The ability to truly feel and understand fullness and emptiness, closing and opening, hardness and softness, stillness in motion, substantial and insubstantial, and yin and yang while practicing (whether forms, weapons, Push Hands, or sparring) is the mark of an accomplished and proficient tai ji quan practitioner.

Shen Ming 神明

Cultivating a spirit that is calm, happy, relaxed, and free to use flowing techniques at will is the third step in mastering tai ji quan, and it could require an entire life time. The highest levels of tai ji quan are seen in those who use the martial art as the desired way of their entire lives. In all their actions they exhibit the ability to change freely from fast to slow, from hard to soft, and from appearing to disappearing. Their hardness lies in softness, and their stillness is seen in motion and yet there is motion in their stillness. They display yin in the yang and yang in the yin, in a great range but always in a peaceful manner.

One need not become one of the immortals of legend who can fly over walls, walk on water, and overpower any opponent. Tai ji quan practice will simply allow one to be calmer, have more patience, think more clearly, resist distraction, be more focused, and generally feel more alive and successful. Real tai ji quan masters are those who manage their lives in a true tai ji way, which makes their spirit light and rich. Everything in their life is balanced. Tai ji quan integrates all the elements of life into its practice. Movement, meditation, martial arts, and spirituality all become a method of exploring one's life and understanding oneself and one's relationship to the universe.

Chinese Terminology for Tai Ji Quan

Philosophy and History 哲学 和 历史

tai ji 太极	Yin and yang balance
wu wei 无为	Principle of non-action
wu ji 无极	Principle of emptiness
Lao Zi 老子	Ancient patriarch of Taoism
Zhuang Zi 庄子	Ancient Taoist philosopher
Zhang San Feng 张三丰	Legendary patriarch of tai ji quan
yin 阴	The feminine principle
yang 阳	The masculine principle
Yi Jing (I Ching) 易经	Book of Changes
ba gua 八卦	Eight trigrams
qian 乾	Heaven
kun 坤	Earth
kan 坎	Water
li 离	Fire
sun 馔	Wind
zhen 震	Thunder
dui 兑	Lake
gen 艮	Mountain
wu xing 五行	Five elements
jin 金	Metal
mu 木	Wood
shui 水	Water
hou 火	Fire
tu 土	Earth

Body Parts and Positions 身体部位和运动姿势

tou 头	Head
yan 眼	Eye
bi 鼻	Nose
zui 嘴	Mouth
er 耳	Ear
shou 手	Hand
shou zhi 手指	Finger
zhang 掌	Palm
quan 拳	Fist
zhou 肘	Elbow
shou bi 手臂	Arm
jian 肩	Shoulder
xiong 胸	Chest
yao 腰	Waist
bei 背	Back
kua 胯	Pelvic area
tui 腿	Leg
jiao 脚	Foot
wan 腕	Wrist
gong bu 弓步	Bow stance or front stance
ma bu 马步	Horse stance
pu bu 仆步	Crouching stance
xu bu 虚步	Empty stance
du li bu 独立步	Crane stance
xie bu 歇步	Cross stance
yang 仰	Leaning backward
fu 伏	Leaning forward
qian 前	Front
hou 后	Back

zuo 左	Left
you 右	Right
gao 高	High
di 低	Low
zhong 中	Middle or medium
zheng 正	Central equilibrium
xie 斜	Leaning
zhan 站	Standing
zuo 坐	Sitting
jin 进	Step forward
tui 退	Step backward
zhuan 转	Turn
tiao 跳	Jump
dun 蹲	Squatting down
zhan zhuang 站桩	Basic standing posture
dan tian 丹田	The area from one to three inches blow the navel, including the acupuncture points of RN4, RN5, and RN6

Tai Ji Quan Techniques 太极拳技术

wu shu 武术	Martial arts
jing 精	Energy essence
qi (chi) 气	Life force
shen 神	Spirit
yi 意	Mind, intent
nei jia quan 内家拳	Internal martial arts
wai jia quan 外家 拳	External martial arts
song 松	Looseness, softness
rou 柔	Softness
chen 沉	Sink
xu 虚	Insubstantial

shi 实	Substantial
shuang zhong 双重	Double weighting
jin 劲	Strength
li 力	Power
fa li (fa jin) 发力	Energy release or release power
tao lu 套路	Form
jian 剑	Sword
jian zhi 剑指	Sword finger
tui shou 推手	Push Hands
san da 散打	Free sparring with punch, kick, throw
qing 轻	Light
zhong 重	Heavy
sui 随	Yielding
nian 黏	Sticking
shen 伸	Expansion
suo 缩	Compression
peng 掤	Ward Off
lu 捋	Roll Back
ji 挤	Press
an 按	Push
cai 采	Pull
lie 挒	Split
zhou 肘	Elbow strike
kao 靠	Shoulder strike
jing zuo 静坐	Meditation
zhao shu 着熟	Knowing skills
dong jin 懂劲	Understanding internal power
shen ming 神明	Spiritual enlightenment

ACKNOWLEDGMENTS

WE ESPECIALLY WISH TO THANK Master Li Bing Ci, the president of the Beijing Northern Wu Style Tai Ji Quan Association and the chief representative of the fourth generation of the Northern Wu Style lineage. With more than fifty years of practicing and teaching experience, he teaches the art with a very rich knowledge and in an easily understood manner. The high skill level and generous teaching style of Master Li Bing Ci have made this book possible.

We also wish to thank Amy Echart for her excellent photography in the Push Hands and martial applications sections. Also, thank you, Brian Kelly, Bill Pagano, xTerri "Metal-Tiger" Ferrari and Donavon Withers for modeling in this book with hearts that understand the true meaning of tai ji quan.

Our thanks also go to our friend Jess O'Brien who professionally suggested we write this book. We want to thank North Atlantic/Blue Snake Books for their support in making the dream of having this book published a realization. The wonderful work and endless patience of our editors Anastasia McGhee and Winn Kalmon, and designer Susan Quasha are deeply appreciated.

ABOUT THE AUTHORS

Tina Chunna Zhang

TINA CHUNNA ZHANG has experienced Chinese martial arts and dance since her childhood in Beijing, China. She moved to the U.S. in the 1980s. She has studied and trained with famous internal martial arts masters both in China and in the U.S. She is a fifth-generation practitioner of Northern Wu Style Tai Ji Quan, training directly under Master Li Bing Ci. She won gold medals in sparring at the Summer Bash Chinese Martial Arts Championships in 2001 and 2002. She has continued to participate and win numerous medals in martial arts tournaments in China and in the U.S. every year; she is a nationally ranked medalist in tai ji quan and ba gua zhang in forms, weapons, and Push Hands. In August 2005, Tina won the national championship in women's Wu Style Tai Ji Quan at the Wu Shu Union National Championship tournament in Las Vegas, Nevada.

Serving as a cultural bridge between the East and West, Tina actively teaches Classical Northern Wu Style Tai Ji Quan and ba gua zhang at the Wu Tang Physical Cultural Association internal martial arts studio and various sports clubs and fitness gyms in New York City. In summer, she teaches during annual retreats at the Healing Tao University in Catskill, New York. She also teaches workshops in Greece, Germany, England, and Ireland. As a professional tai ji quan instructor and personal trainer, she has helped many people achieve physical and emotional health and fitness goals through her training methods. Along with the internal martial arts, Tina specializes in weight control, flexibility, women's health, self-defense, and energy therapy.

For more information about Tina Chunna Zhang, please visit the website www.earthqigong.com.

Frank Allen

FRANK ALLEN has studied and practiced the internal energy arts since 1973. He was an early student of Master B. P. Chan, from whom he learned the internal martial arts of ba gua zhang, xing yi quan, and tai ji quan, as well as the healing art of qi gong. Frank began to study with Master B. K. Frantzis in 1976 and over the next two and a half decades studied Frantzis's internal martial arts, including Wu Style Tai Ji Quan, nei gong, and Taoist meditation. He has also studied the internal martial arts with Master Jiang Jian Yee. When on his training trips to Beijing, China, Frank is the tai ji student of Northern Wu Style Tai Ji Quan Grandmaster Li Bing Ci and studies Classical Cheng Style Ba Gua Zhang with  Grandmaster Liu Jing Ru. Since 1984 Frank has been the disciple of Western Boxing Master Verne "The Bulldog" Williams. Frank was the first person ever certified to teach the ba gua of B. K. Frantzis and has been certified to teach ba gua and tai ji quan by Jiang Jian Ye.

In 1979 Frank founded the Wu Tang Physical Culture Association in New York City, with branches in Southern California, Middletown, New York, and Frankfurt, Germany. Over the years the Wu Tang PCA has produced many tournament champions and a core of competent instructors.

Frank has authored more than thirty articles for the major martial arts and Taoist related periodicals in the U.S and has self-published on Celtic Taoism. He and the Wu Tang PCA video production crew have produced twelve instructional videos covering the subjects of ba gua zhang, tai ji quan, xing yi quan, Taoist philosophy, meditation, and the Fighting for Health system.

Frank teaches workshops around the U.S. and in Europe, as well as his regular classes in New York. He has been the internal martial arts instructor of Healing Tao University summer retreats since 1999, and in 2005 started a joint Healing Tao University-Wu Tang PCA ba gua zhang instructor certification program.

For more information about Frank Allen, please visit the website www.wutang-pca.com.